D1592738

Sexual Abuse of Power
in the
Black Church

Sexual Misconduct in the
African American Churches

Donald H. Matthews, PhD

WESTBOW
PRESS
A DIVISION OF THOMAS NELSON

ISBN: 978-1-4497-4323-9 (sc)
ISBN: 978-1-4497-4324-6 (e)
ISBN: 978-1-4497-4325-3 (hc)
Library of Congress Control Number: 2012904837

WestBow Press books may be ordered through booksellers or by contacting:

WestBow Press
A Division of Thomas Nelson
1663 Liberty Drive
Bloomington, IN 47403
www.westbowpress.com
1-(866) 928-1240

Printed in the United States of America

WestBow Press rev. date: 5/04/2012

Dedication

This book is dedicated to:

Dr. James M. Gustafson, my Ethics Professor, and
Rev. William J. Vance, MA, spiritual mentor.
Ms. Esther Belle Henderson (deceased)
Rev. Dr. Robert D. Hill, BD, DDIV (deceased)
Ms. Jeanette Branch, MSW (deceased)

My role models, friends and colleagues. We will meet again.

Contents

A Letter to Black Pastors

Dear Pastors:

You have been called to the most responsible position in the African American community. You are the inheritors of the legacy of some of the most admired and talented agents of God's mercy and love that history has ever seen. The works of Martin Luther King, Jr. Minister Malcolm X El-Shabazz, Dr. Benjamin E. Mays and many, many, more; too many to name preceded you in the struggle for freedom and justice for the poor and oppressed black community. You have been charged with caring for "the widows and the orphans" and like Jesus, you are to show compassion to all women who have been treated negatively by the double standard of patriarchal power. (woman taken in adultery; woman that bathed Jesus' feet).

Your ministerial exemplars have been role models for freedom fighters around the world and stand as shining lights for the youth of this nation and the world. These men taught us of the power that lies in the witness of The African American Church. However, many of our male leaders were not faithful to the gospel of love and compassion to our sisters in need. In issues of human sexuality the church should have be without fault or stain but it has been difficult to realize that noble goal.

The oppressive historical situation of unbridled sexual, economic and racial oppression has contributed to an African American Church that has not developed a sexual ethic that cares for and keeps safe those who are the least powerful in our midst.

This has been especially true for females in the community. However, we now have the benefits of a human rights struggle and the education so that religious leaders can learn to develop appropriate relationships with female members in our communities of faith and worship. Since females represent the overwhelming majority in number, if not in power, often approaching 80% if the total congregation, it is time for justice, respect and true love to prevail.

I wrote this book first of all to try and protect the persons in your congregations who may become the victims of the sexualized abuse of power. These victims have traditionally been women due to the overwhelming heterosexual orientation of most of our male pastors who have developed and continue to promote hetero-sexist theological views which see women as sexual objects and less privileged than men. This has led to women and girls remaining the most vulnerable persons who are subject to sexual victimization.

The allegations concerning Bishop Long's abuse of power regarding his relationships with young males now affords us the opportunity to consider the entire spectrum of abuse in which the vast majority of the victims have been girls and women. I believe that it has been the failure of the African American Church to engage in extended and knowledgeable discussions about our views of gender and sexuality that underlies this abusive ideology and practice. Instead of championing a view of liberation and justice that includes justice and care for our women, we have simply adopted a traditional view of sexuality that is strewn with the oppressive cultural scriptural interpretations and folkways that are patriarchal, materialistic and hetero-sexist. But just as we were able to see freedom when reading the Bible when the majority of Christians saw slavery; we can also see sexual and gender equality where others have read the oppression and domination of women. Unfortunately, this ideology of gender oppression was not only present among Christian evangelicals when Africans were brought to America, it was also found among those African leaders who conspired with Euro-Americans to sell us into slavery.

But, as free and rational religious leaders we can develop interpretations of scripture that reinforce the sexual equality of women that is nascent, though not fully realized, in Western scriptural traditions. For example, though most of us recognize that even though the New Testament scripture states that adultery is the only reason for divorce, we now recognize and will perform marriage ceremonies for those who have received divorces for other reasons. This is because we believe that the highest law, the law of love, which is not a law but an attitude of compassion, leads us to recognize that there are other grounds for divorce that are consistent with the law of love. We no longer believe, as the early church did, that women are the heirs of Eve's disobedience and therefore must be dominated by men.

We know that early Christian theologians thought that the "original sin" of Adam and Eve was the knowledge of sexuality. This interpretation resulted in a negative view of the body and sexuality and we are still reaping the consequences of that negative interpretation of sexuality. We now recognize the beauty of sexuality when used appropriately and with love; and no longer think of sexuality solely in terms of lust, as was the case with the early Church Fathers.

These are just two instances where the continuing role of biblical interpretation under the guidance of God's love can restore and renew our sacred communities so that gender and sexual equality can be realized. I have faith that we can develop different notions regarding sexuality and eliminate sexual abuse in our Churches. This book outlines where I think we developed this destructive ideology of sexual abuse and provides suggestions for the development of a code of sexual ethics that is just and compassionate. We must discuss this code among ourselves and our congregations and hold one another accountable in a spirit of love and responsibility if we want to avoid the continued harm and scandal which has affected so many of our members and clergy.

Up to this day African American Liberation theology has largely ignored the ways in which African Americans oppress each other. It has rarely examined or acknowledged the presence of internal contradictions that are the basis for our continued oppression. Dr. Alvin Poussaint's book; "Why Blacks Kill Blacks," is one of those works that boldly stated that it was the oppression of black women by Civil Rights and Black Power leaders that killed the Movements from within. If we are to be free we must acknowledge our spiritual poverty that has resulted in our being our own worst enemies. This letter and book is not written in a spirit of condemnation but of hope as we recognize, confess and repent of our failings and faults in this area of our communal life. As a minister of the gospel, and more importantly as a child of God, I have the faith to believe that with the proper education and support we can turn the corner and become role models for those who will come after us.

We had the misfortune of being the unknowing victims of centuries of silence concerning sexuality that was originally meant to protect us from the prying eyes of a larger society which feared, but was also fascinated, by African American bodies and Black sexuality. It is time for us to "keep it real" and use the intelligence and wisdom that God gives us to openly explore these issues with fellow clergy and community members knowing that none are perfect but all are seeking a higher level of perfection and sanctification. In doing so we must also recognize the ways in which we have been victimized as well. Our macho positions as authority figures must not blind us into thinking that we have been untouched by abuse and neglect.

I hope that this book will help us on our way.

Sincerely,
Your Brother,
Rev. Dr. Don Matthews

Introduction

There have been dozens if not hundreds of books written regarding the subject of sexual abuse in the church in the last thirty years but none about sexual abuse in the Black Church. Is this because sexual abuse does not occur in the Black Church? ***On the contrary, a recent study discovered that black females are likely to experience three times the amount of sexual abuse as females in white churches.*** This book is an attempt to raise this issue and discuss this problem with the Black Church specifically in mind. This problem has been hidden for several reasons that this book will address. It is important to recognize the suffering of African Americans in this area and to try and remedy it as well. This cannot be done as long as the sexual taboo of discussing sexual matters continues in the African American community and churches.

This book is based on over forty years of participation, service and observation in black churches; thirty of which happened during my tenure as a minister and scholar of African American religion. My Ph.D and Masters of Divinity degrees in the areas of The Sociology and Psychology of Religion, with a specialty in Ethics, were awarded respectively from The Divinity School of the University of Chicago; and The Pacific School of Religion in Berkeley California's Graduate Theological Union. I consider my work to exist in the lineage of scholars and ministers like Dr. Benjamin E. Mays and Dr. Robert Franklin. They were two of the former and present Presidents of Morehouse College in Atlanta who also earned their doctorates at The Divinity School of the University of Chicago. These scholars evidenced a keen interest in promoting the spiritual growth of Black religious and community leaders. Among others Dr. Mays was extremely influential in the spiritual formation of Rev. Dr. Martin Luther King, Jr. His book; Born to Rebel is an American religious classic. I also had the rare privilege and honor of taking a course in Black Theology when Dr. Franklin was a faculty member at The Divinity School. His current leadership at Morehouse is breaking new ground on issues of sexuality and gender in the black church and community.

Background

I was reminded of the importance of this project when I relocated to California for a year where I was to begin a clinical residence year in pastoral psychotherapy and counseling. I had previously gone to seminary in Berkeley, California and since most of my children and grandchildren lived in that area I thought it would be an ideal place to kill two birds with one stone. I could gain my clinical certification as well as have more opportunity to spend time with my family. I was assigned as the Chaplain to the Mental Health Ward of the hospital where I did the bulk of my supervised clinical practicum.

In this role I had the opportunity to minister to many persons who had been affected by the issue of sexual abuse as well as a host of other mental health issues. This issue also confronted me unexpectedly, but directly, as I searched for housing in the area. I contacted several churches in close proximity to the hospital for assistance in my quest for housing and found myself in touch with a minister whom I had met while I was in seminary some twenty five years earlier. He was now the interim pastor at a church that was just down the street from the hospital that I served. The church was in a state of decline and he was charged with providing leadership until the next full time minister could be installed. When he learned that I was coming to the area he suggested that we meet to discuss the state of the church with the incoming minister. In addition to my first book; "Honoring the Ancestors: An African Cultural Interpretation of Black Religion and Literature", (Oxford University Press 1998) I had also written a book on churches that were in decline "Can This Church Live? A Church, Its Neighborhood and Social Transformation," (Pilgrim Press, 2004; Wipf & Stock, 2010). I was therefore open to discussing the issues that were confronting this particular church.

I met with my old colleague and the new minister but there seemed to be something that was hanging in the air that was preventing us from engaging in a true dialogue concerning the church. I felt like I was a counselor in a family therapy session in which a family secret was held but not acknowledged. Family therapists have long recognized that it is what is hidden or un-stated that often holds the burden of responsibility for the family dysfunction. But it may also hold the key for the healing of the family system. I left the meeting not feeling that we had really communicated and put the meeting in the back of my mind.

I eventually found a place to stay through the gracious invitation of an extremely generous woman who happened to be a former member of that church. She was now worshiping at another church in the area where she was currently on the Board of Trustees. When I mentioned my conversation with the pastors her response was muted and matter of fact. It was only later, in a conversation with another colleague who had also attended the same seminary with me, that I learned why their responses were so similarly ambiguous.

He told me that this particular church had become famous, or rather infamous, for the sexual misconduct of its pastor. In fact, this particular church had been used as a case study as an example of a church that had experienced severe decline after having enormous success. He talked about it as being the leading example of a successful and thriving church becoming the poster child for the organizational decline of many churches due to the misconduct of its pastoral leader. Apparently, that abusing pastor of that church was a charismatic minister who had overseen the tremendous expansion of the church until it became one of the largest and most influential churches in the nation. However once the pastor's sexual abuse of power became known to the congregation it led to the eventual destruction of the church. Church members took sides for or against the pastor and also against each other. The pastor's abuse of power with numerous female church members eventually led to a large scale exodus by members who felt that their trust had been betrayed.

When I remember the countenance of that kind and gracious woman who had allowed me to live in her parental home I now recognize a sense of pathos and sadness that accompanied her discretion. Her sense of silent sadness was also what I experienced when I had the meeting with the pastors of that church. This kind of sexual abuse of power represents a deep betrayal and leaves a woundedness and pain that has long lasting and lingering effects that may never be fully healed. The pastoral abuse of power does not only negatively affect the persons directly and intimately involved with the pastor in his misconduct. It also has a harmful effect on the entire church. It was to her credit that my benefactor did not turn her back on the Christian church and she continued her faithful service in another church setting. I am sure many persons were not able to weather the storm and left not only that church but the Christian church in general in response to the hypocrisy of the sexual abuse of power by their pastoral leader.

After teaching courses in ethics and human sexuality in the Black community at seminaries and universities for over twenty years I realized that there was little or no information concerning the Black Church and sexual abuse. I knew first hand of many Black Churches in which sexual abuse had occurred but the violations had usually been met with silence or other resistance to dealing with the issue. The publicized case of Bishop Eddie Long in Atlanta is a classic example of the denial process that is in place in Black Churches when confronted with the issue of sexual misconduct in the church. In my long experience of teaching about ethics and sexuality in the Black community I had come to several conclusions about the origins of sexual abuse and misconduct in the Black churches; why it was permitted, sometimes encouraged, and rarely discussed or punished. This book is an attempt to address this situation of silence and abuse regarding the sexual misconduct of pastors in the Black Church with the hope that it can help to prevent the continuation of these practices.

Chapter One

Sexual Abuse In The Church

I identify two major psychological conditions that contribute to the sexual abuse of power by pastors and other religious leaders in the church. These two conditions are 1) Sexual Boundary Violations; and 2) Sexual Perversions. These are not exclusive categories. Persons who have difficulty maintaining appropriate boundaries with others can also be engaged in sexual perversions. Persons who are sexually perverted are by definition violating the boundaries of others.

The psychological process that underlies these two conditions is the psychological and spiritual need for power over others. Sexual abuse is one expression of this need for power. It may be due to some unresolved emotional or psychological issues that can be caused by any number of factors. The pastor may have an overwhelming need to help others that blinds him to his needs to maintain appropriate boundaries. There may be the presence of unresolved psychological issues caused by the trauma of family dysfunction; or social interactions that have left the pastor with a need to humiliate others as he himself was humiliated. It may be due to low self- esteem leading to a need to feel wanted. The reasons are particular to the particular person. These issues must not be used as excuses for misconduct. However, recognition of these issues and their effect are the key to the prevention of abuse and the treatment of the abuser.

Ethically speaking, any behavior in which a person is used as an object is abusive. In this case it involves using a person for one's own sexual gratification despite the negative effects involved in that behavior. The pastor who engages in sexual misconduct with his members is engaging in activity in which his power as a spiritual leader is misused for reasons that are ultimately harmful to him, his victim, his church, and his family. The entire system of church and family are harmed by his abusive actions.

Because the pastor is the primary role model and leader of the congregation he sets the terms by example for ethical or un-ethical behavior in the church. His actions will have a profound effect on the spiritual and psychological well-being of his church and community. Although all instances of the sexual abuse of power is deplorable and damaging, it is especially true when this behavior takes place with under-aged youth. Therefore, the first condition that I will address is the issue of sexual perversion in the form of sexual molestation of young people in the church. The first two narratives concern this expression of sexual abuse in the Black church.

Narratives of Sexual Abuse of Children and Youth
Rape of a Youth in the Church Office

This story was told to me by a forty year old woman who is the mother of four children. She was a devoted member of her church and was active in the choir and other activities. However, as she became more educated she was dissatisfied with the power relation in the church that did not allow her and other women to serve in positions of authority. As I got to know her she revealed the sexual abuse she had suffered in her family and the church. This is her story.

"When I was eight I was subject to sexual abuse by my stepfather. I recently had a flashback in which I remembered hearing my mother tell her husband, my stepfather, not to hurt me as he came into my room to violate me. I dreaded being left alone with him because I knew what would happen. This abuse changed me from a happy go lucky child to a moody kid who began to withdraw into a shell. I was only able to be myself when I went to live with my grandmother

during the summers. Even then I was afraid that he was doing the same thing to my younger sisters. I know I sound like Celie from the Color Purple but the reason why the movie was so loved by so many black women is because it represented much of what we suffered.

Finally I got old enough to protect myself and threatened to kill him if he ever touched me again. When I complained about his behavior to my mother when I was younger she beat me severely and accused me of being "fast" and encouraging his actions. I knew that when I got older and stronger it would be up to me to defend myself from his advances. Even though I was finally able to defend myself my mother recognized that I was still depressed. Like most black women she was suspicious of mental health professionals and didn't want her husband to face the legal system.

Instead, she took me to receive counseling from the pastor of the church when I turned twelve. I had blossomed early and I had large breasts which brought me a lot of unwanted sexual attention from males. Unfortunately, this was also true of the pastor. Instead of counseling me he told me that it was his duty to heal me from the rape and sexual abuse. He told me the only way that could happen is if he was able to show me how to do it right. This led to several petting sessions on the couch in his study which eventually led to sexual intercourse. I still remember feeling disgusted and afraid as he penetrated me in the name of the Lord. I can still see the picture of Jesus looking down on us as he raped me on his couch in his study.

Even though I was afraid that my mother would have the same reaction she had when I told on my stepfather I finally refused to see him anymore and told my mother why. Much to my surprise my mother supported my decision with a look of sorrow and hurt in her eyes. The man she had looked up to and given her trust turned out to be just as immoral as her husband. She reported his behavior to the church officials but instead of confronting the pastor they accused me of lying. When my allegations became known I was approached by several other young girls who had suffered the same mistreatment. To this day I am filled with anger at the thought that the church which was supposed to protect me and guide me turned on me in order to protect their spiritual leader from harm. I wonder how many other girls he had violated over the course of a thirty year ministry. He is now one of the respected senior pastors in the Kansas City area. When I see him it is all I can do to stop from gaining my revenge. But nobody cares about the troubles of black women. We are supposed to be able to protect ourselves and when we can't or don't because we don't know better or because of what we've been told we become the victims.

When I needed help the pastor let me down. When my mother finally sought out help for me the church let us down. This has had profound negative consequences for my life. I began to think that I deserved to be treated like a toilet for black men to piss on. I've been raped three times. I contracted several STD's and sometimes I have to drink before I can feel comfortable doing it. This has left me with a damaged liver and other health problems. I don't have the strength to change my life. I can only hope and pray that my kids won't have the same problems."

Sexual Abuse of a Child by a Church Official

The previous story was not the only time I had heard about the rape and sexual abuse of young girls by their spiritual leaders. While I was teaching at one Seminary on the East Coast I heard more stories about this and other kinds of sexual abuses by black pastors. The seminary held a yearly conference for ministers. Some of the most prominent Baptist pastors in the country would attend in order to gain continuing education and to mentor younger seminarians in to the ways of the ministry.

At one such conference there were several black female seminarians who had received the call to preach and who were intending to serve the church. After lunch there was a session that was dedicated to speaking about gender relationships in the Baptist congregations. Several of the women knew of many instances of sexual abuse in the church and so they raised that as a question at the conference.

The ensuing discussion revealed how little consciousness these seasoned and experienced ministers had of the destructive role that they and their peers had been playing in their churches. This culminating story brought the house down as one of the more prominent ministers attempted to show how understanding, helpful and compassionate he had been when dealing with this problem. He told us how one of his Deacons had sexually abused one of the adolescent girls in the church. This particular church official had been given the charge of training the young people to serve the communion and welcome visitors to the church on Sunday morning. This prominent minister recounted how he had received a complaint from one of the mothers of an adolescent girl who was a part of the Deacon's group. The mother reported that the Deacon had attempted to force her child to have sexual relations with him. The mother was a single mother who looked for the church to provide a sense of home and safety for her girl and when her daughter reported this problem to her she took it to the pastor.

The minister proudly told us that after he received this complaint he called the Deacon into his office and confronted him with his abusive activities. The Deacon confessed to his misconduct and begged the pastor for forgiveness. The pastor related that he then forgave the Deacon and told him that he would be suspended for a month while he counseled with the pastor on how to control his sexual behavior. The pastor told us that when the mother realized that this was all that the pastor was going to do to correct the situation she complained to the Pastor and the Deacon Board but was rebuffed. Instead of filing charges, and in order to spare her daughter from more humiliation and abuse, she and her daughter left the church in disgust.

When the women seminarians and others of us heard this story we were appalled and let out a collective cry of protest. Several people informed the minister that the Deacon committed a criminal act and should have been prosecuted and at least reported to the authorities. They also said that the church should have offered to provide counseling and medical treatment for the young girl so that she could heal from the trauma that the Deacon had caused.

I will never forget the look of pain and bewilderment on the pastor's face when he heard the response. He was actually expecting the audience to applaud him for his treatment of the situation. When I asked him and the other ministers present to define sexual abuse or misconduct they had no idea. Upon reflection they explained that abuse was a "white" or a "legal" term that had no place in the Black church.

Interpreting the Narratives:
Pastor as Sexual Predator

Anti-Psychological Bias

The previous narratives reveal acts of power that are perverse in nature. Child molestation has no place in the church or family. The presence of an anti-Psychological Bias in Black churches has contributed to this problem. One of the reasons why it has been so difficult for the black community to deal with this issue is due to the well-known and documented anti-psychological stance of the black community. There is some justification for this suspicion of psychology due to past tendencies of the helping professions to use models of psychological development that did not take into account the social and psychological cultural characteristics of African Americans. It was not unusual for sociologists and psychologists to label black behavior as deviant if blacks exhibited family structures or behavior that did not meet the standard white middle class cultural norms. For a long time there was also a lack of qualified helping professionals in the black community which meant that persons and families suffering psychologically based trauma and illnesses had little opportunity for treatment. Instead of seeking professional psychological help the tendency was to resort to the church or other folk based remedies to deal with instances of mental problems and illnesses.

One woman related how she was almost the victim of a sexual attack by her younger brother. Her response to him was that he should find a girlfriend so that he could exercise his sexual needs. When she reported the incident to their mother the family felt as though they had no available resources to address her family's situation. When she spoke to her son she simply asked him if he had something he wanted to say concerning the incident with his sister. He replied no and that was the end of the matter. When I spoke with the young man years later he told of how his sister had continually exposed herself to him which led to his attempt to have sex with her. A competent family therapist could have helped the family to understand the reasons for his and his sister's behavior and helped the family work through their issues.

Unfortunately, this history of mistrust and lack of adequate psychological care and therapy has led to a tendency to throw the baby out with the bath water. It is evident from my many years of study and training in Depth Psychology that a psychological understanding of human development is essential toward helping the Black community understand and deal with this issue. Now that there are many qualified Black and non-Black therapists who are more aware of the psychological and social dynamics of the African American community Black churches and families have greater access to competent therapeutic resources.

When I taught and directed the Black Church Community Programs at Chicago Theological Seminary we invited Marian Wright Edelman, the Director of the Children's Defense Fund and the foremost advocate of the needs of children in America, to speak at a conference. The conference was heavily attended by African American church women who were in the various helping professions as teachers, social workers, nurses and the like. However, few of their pastors were in attendance. It was apparent that those who were on the front lines in treating and working with black children and families were black women who had a strong spiritual foundation and who were also equipped with psychological knowledge. It also suggested that their pastors were at least one stepped removed from the suffering of the children and families in their community and were much less prepared to deal with their psychological issues. The churches must find ways of bringing these two groups together for the benefit of the African American community.

As more blacks, especially black pastors, receive more psychological and pastoral psychological training more black community members and pastors will receive the emotional help they need. This anti-psychological bias seems to be lessening but in most of my interaction with the black community there is still a lack of trust and a suspicion of using "white" methods, meaning psychology, to interpret and treat the abusive behavior of black people. This anti-psychological bias also exists among the educated and non-educated black clergy. In teaching classes in human sexuality and the black community I found it difficult to get black clergy to understand the importance of issues of emotional and psychological boundaries. A helping professional, and especially a minister, who does not understand these issues makes him or herself vulnerable to engaging in an abuse of power.

Black churches must be open to the possibility that they have hired someone who is not psychologically fit to be a minister. The silence around sexual issues may mean that many clergy have been hired without proper screening by hiring committees. This lack of oversight and the silence regarding sexuality in general in the black church, may contribute to the fact that many instances of sexual abuse by ministers may be unreported, ignored or excused.

Confusion of Homosexual Behavior with Child Abuse

There is no reason to think that black persons are any less susceptible to emotional illnesses which may lead to their committing acts of sexual coercion and sexual violence. Black pastors share the same human faults as do others. There are black clergy who are sexual predators and who use their position to prey on trusting, unsuspecting victims.

The well-publicized cases of sexual abuse in the Catholic Church are not confined to the Catholic Church. One of the problems in the black community is that there is a tendency to see issues of the sexual abuse of children as the result of these priests' status as celibates. I have heard many members state that if the Catholic church would just allow their priests to get married and engage in sexual relations then they wouldn't need to abuse young boys. This is an example of the lack of clarity regarding issues of sexual abuse of power in the black community. This same lack of clarity was seen in comments regarding the Eddie Long case. Many critics of Long were more concerned with allegations of his homosexuality than the possibility of his abuse of power.

One of my most frustrating teaching moments while teaching seminary students occurred when I had several pastors in my class on sexuality and they insisted that these priests abused children because they were homosexual. Because they believed that homosexuality was a grievous sin they confused homosexual activity with the homosexual abuse of male children. What they didn't seem to realize, or want to understand, is that priests or ministers who are child molesters are emotionally ill and that their sexual orientation does not contribute to their abusive behavior. There are undoubtedly more straight sexual predators that there are gay perpetrators. I later discovered that one of the pastors was the victim of rape while he was in jail. This traumatic incident was now affecting his attitude toward homosexuality since he had not worked through the effects of his own sexual victimization.

I have talked with many persons in the black community who do not distinguish between issues of homosexual behavior and that of child abuse. They have a tendency to act and believe as if they are one and the same issue. In fact, heterosexual pastors are much more likely to engage in sexually abusive behavior. This linking of child abuse with homosexuality may be a way of black pastors justifying their anti-gay attitudes and hiding their own instances of sexual abuse with female children and adults in their churches. Once again, these two issues are not related and there is no evidence to suggest that gay persons are more prone to sexually abuse children. Furthermore, modern psychology no longer classifies homosexual orientation as a psychopathological condition.

In one situation I preached a sermon in a large middle class black church in which I examined the biblical admonitions against same sex behavior. I demonstrated that close study of the texts revealed no understanding of the idea of sexual orientation as we understand it today, and that there have been numerous misinterpretations of biblical passages that were supposedly anti-gay.

The next Sunday one of the church officials grabbed the microphone and attempted to prevent me from speaking due to my refusal to condemn homosexuals. He eventually had to be restrained and removed from the church building so that the service could continue. I found it instructive that the next week it was discovered that he was a frequent customer of young prostitutes in his neighborhood. It was almost a textbook case of persons being disturbed about homosexuality because they were having difficulties in their own sexual life.

I have found that there is a general ignorance among the black churches regarding the biblical interpretations of texts regarding sexuality and homosexuality. Instead of availing themselves of the best of biblical scholarship regarding biblical interpretations in these areas they rely on interpretations that are either not accurate translations of the texts in question; or have been subject to intentional or accidental misinterpretations and translations.

What is not generally understood in much of the black church community is that it is not the sexual orientation of the clergy that is driving the behavior of sexual abuse. Instead, the behavior is being driven by the sexual abuser's desire to gain power over his victim. The sexually abusive behavior is the means the abusive pastor uses that fulfills an emotional need of the sexual predator to humiliate his victim. The abuse is related to the desire for power, and as some experts in sexual abuse would say, the sexual abuse of power is not primarily about sex, it is about the abuser gaining a sense of power through abusing the less powerful victim.

I believe that it is more comprehensive to say that sexual abuse involves both sex and power, especially when sexual perversion is involved. The perpetrator has the desire to gain power by humiliating the victim through coercion, seduction or force, and the feelings associated with sexual dominance and coercion feeds his need for power over others. Denial becomes an issue as the perpetrator justifies his actions as due to external or internal forces beyond their control or due to some fault of his victims.

Poor Emotional Boundaries and Sexual Abuse

This next section deals with the problems of sexual misconduct as they are related to religious leaders failing to maintain appropriate emotional and sexual boundaries. My observation is that this is the major dynamic that is responsible for most acts of sexual abuse in the church. I will present several examples of how poor and undefined boundaries lead to sexual misconduct. By poor emotional boundaries I mean that the pastor or religious leader does not maintain enough emotional, physical and sexual distance between their own needs and those of their followers. This can lead to inappropriate sexual relationships with persons whom they are supposed to be leading. This often takes the form of multiple and or adulterous relationships with church members. I believe that it so common as to almost be normative. So much so that it has become a living dynamic and has developed its own discourse that justifies un-ethical behavior.

Violation of Emotional/Sexual Boundaries

Clergy are involved in the most emotionally intimate levels of human relationships as they discuss major life issues with their parishioners. This can create feelings of closeness and familiarity which can easily lead to an overstepping of emotional boundaries. Here again the history of silence about sexuality works against the black pastor. As I will discuss later there has been the development of an entire ethos and ethics around issues of sexuality in the black community that serves to heighten the possibility of a failure for adequate boundary setting.

In addition, the anti-psychological bias leads black pastors and parishioners to deny the importance of adequate boundaries in favor of folk beliefs and knowledge that may have been functional at one time but are no longer adequate to prevent the sexual abuse of power. This folk knowledge may in fact be a warped imitation, reproduction. and replication of the sexual and psychological oppression that blacks have experienced at the hands of a racist society.

The Discourse of Sexual Abuse

The idea that pastors should expect to have sexual relationships with their parishioners are common among black clergy and church persons. They have convinced themselves that it is "natural" for clergy, in most cases male clergy, to violate appropriate sexual boundaries. This folk perspective is thought to be an alternative to more puritanical white views of sexuality. In fact, these ideas are not derived from an African past but they are in fact the recapitulation of the lack of sexual boundaries experienced by blacks during slavery. The sexual violation of black women, men and children in which slave masters exploited the black body for economic benefit and physical pleasure destroyed family bonds and boundaries that regulated appropriate loving, intimate, and proper sexual activity. African American male slaves were forced to have sexual intercourse with their female community members in order to produce more slave children for commerce and labor on the plantations. This means that black males, as well as females, suffered the destructive effects of the sexual abuse of power. Slave narratives are consistent on this issue as they relate how black males felt violated by the system of slavery which required that they sexually violate their black female community members. What lingering effects that may have had on the black male psyche is open to conjecture but it may have contributed to the present prevalence of the sexual abuse of power by male clergy.

Sexual Practices and Attitudes in Africa

Anyone who has studied the sexual practices of Africans in traditional African societies are struck by their ease with the acceptance of sexual activity and the goodness of the body; but these societies also had in place certain rule and guidelines which protected women and children from exploitation. The body was both erotic and the site for appropriate ethical activity. Some might argue that when African tribal leaders began to abuse their powers in this regard and overstep the traditional boundaries, especially during the time of European colonial exploitation of Africa. This misbehavior and appropriation of patriarchal behavior weakened the community and made the people more vulnerable to exploitation. (Things Fall Apart by Chinua Achebe, Death and the King's Horseman by Wole Soyinke)

Transference; Black Folk Culture; and Ethics

Most professional codes of ethics are built on an acceptance of the need for healthy emotional boundaries between the helping professionals and their clients. This is true of doctors, nurses, lawyers, teachers, etc., but the black church and clergy have developed a folk understanding of sexuality which has relieved them of the responsibility of maintaining appropriate boundaries. It has become too easy to explain abuse of power as simply the result of sexual attraction, community expectations or dubious biblical interpretations.

Most codes of ethics state that there should be a prohibition against sexual contact between the professional and the client. This is important for several reasons. The first reason is because there is a tendency for the person being helped to develop feelings of dependency or attachment (Transference) to the professional who is in a position of power. These are often sexualized feelings in which the client believes that he or she is in love with the helper; and they may project their feelings so that they may believe that this love also exists in the helper toward them. These feelings create an idea that they are special and are the leader's favorite. If the leader is not careful about maintaining appropriate boundaries, the desire for closeness makes the parishioner particularly vulnerable to manipulation and exploitation by the helper who is in a greater power relationship.

This effect, first described by Sigmund Freud is called transference because the client, or in this case, the parishioner, transfers or projects their misplaced feelings of love, affection and sometimes anger or other emotions onto the helper. This is not in and of itself a bad thing. Freud and other depth psychologists believed that there was no healing without transference because it was through transference that the patient revealed their deepest feelings. These feelings could then be used for healing as long as the healer maintained an appropriate emotional, sexual and physical distance from the client and did not give in to these projections of love and closeness.

Counter-transference is when the helper also projects their feelings on to the client and acts in such a manner that violates the boundary between the client and the patient. This is often sexual but it can also take the form of other issues that may be alive in the unconscious of the helper such as treating the parishioner like a spouse, girlfriend, son, daughter or friend. The helper is convinced that the client needs his involvement as a sign that the pastor cares for them and that the parishioner is worthy of love. This is a sign of co-dependent behavior and makes the leader feel special and important.

Pastors who violate these boundaries may often suffer from a narcissistic psychological attitude. I have seen many ministers' ego inflate as they find themselves the center of their parishioner's attention. A classic symptom of narcissism and counter transference is when the pastor develops the idea that only the pastor can help the person in need. This is an important sign to the pastor or helper that he or she is in over her head in a particular relationship.

As I stated before, I have found that a lack of effective boundaries to be the predominant manifestation of abuse of power in most of the cases that I have witnessed or discussed. The pastor and layperson are convinced that there is a real and true attraction that exists between them. I have heard pastors rationalize this state of affairs in many ways that often combined black folk beliefs with psychological issues of dependency and transference. Pastors often use these encounters to boost feelings of self-esteem or importance. But I have yet to see a case in which someone wasn't hurt in this encounter.

Pastor as Helping Professional

Persons not only tend to put their trust in their pastor as a loving and trusted father figure they often come for help from the pastor when they are in emotional need and vulnerability. This has been especially true of black persons due to the paucity of trained counselors and other helping professionals. When I have asked black church members if they would accept this kind of sexual misconduct from a doctor, social worker, policeman or counselor who deals with persons in a state of crisis they are better able to see why it is important for the pastor to also establish clear boundaries. For a pastor or other helping professional to do otherwise would be to take advantage of one's position by exploiting someone who is experiencing emotional difficulty.

Pastor's Role as Father Figure (Projection of Husband and Lover)

In order to continue to discuss this issue as it relates to the black pastor it is first necessary to understand the unique role that the black pastor plays in the black community. The pastor has been more than just a religious leader. The pastor has also been seen as a kind of Father that guides the church. The historical and contemporary destruction of the black family by slavery and historical discrimination has led to the pastor becoming an ever increasing paternal figure in the church and community.

Black mothers have especially looked to the pastor as a role model and substitute father/daddy/role model for their children. Boys and girls who may not have a positive male role model are shown the pastor as the father figure that has been missing in their lives. This is one reason that makes abuse of power such a devastating action. Along with the projection of Father also comes the projection/wish of Husband and Lover. Often women have expected the pastor to play these roles as well. It is not uncommon for black female parishioners to expect their pastor to fulfill their intimate emotional and sexual needs.

I have often heard black females minimize the sexual misconduct of the pastor by claiming that "he is just a man" or that "men with power have always cheated." I have heard many such justifications but when these persons come to understand that they would never tolerate it if a father had sex with his children; or that husbands should have free reign to engage in as many sexual encounters as possible; then they begin to see why a pastoral abuse of power can have such negative consequences.

Helping professionals know that it is common for their patients or clients to develop feelings of love and attachment but it is their responsibility to help the person develop ways to manage their lives that are not based on an emotional dependence with the person who is giving them care. A failure to do so robs the person in crisis from developing emotional skills to deal with their issues and it thereby prolongs or prevents the road to healing. In the next chapter I will continue to explore the patterns of abuse.

Chapter Two

African American Sexual Ethics

This chapter will continue to discuss the many ways that boundary issues surface in the lives of the black community and black churches. They occur in such terrific variation that the common issue of poor boundaries is not always acknowledged or understood.

The Down Low Minister

The "down low" phenomenon is the hiding of same sex sexual preferences by black males from their families and communities in order to avoid the likelihood of social rejection and oppression. I found the down low black minister to be pervasive in the community regardless of region. When I taught a class on Human Sexuality and the Black Community in a Midwestern city, one of my students related how her husband had been a minister and a pillar of one of the local congregations. She was having difficulty in her marriage and discovered that her husband was cheating on her with other women in the church. She informed him that she knew that he had the failings of most men and that she was willing to remain in the marriage but that it was important that he protect himself and not to endanger her life by bringing home STDs or HIV-AIDS.

However, one day she returned home earlier than expected and found him in bed with a male lover. He had not informed her that he was bisexual. She ordered him and his lover out of her house before their children came home and announced to him that their marriage was over. She was not only disappointed with his lack of respect and discretion by having his lover come to their family home. The fact that he was a minister who preached against homosexuality, and that he was exposing her to the possibility of HIV due to his failure to use protection during his sexual activities was a breach of trust that she could not accept. His hypocrisy and deception as she put it "had taken away my choice."

She immediately sued for divorce. He begged her to forgive him and complained to his fellow ministers that his wife was divorcing him for no good reason. His ministerial colleagues, their wives and congregation began to pressure her to reconsider but she was resolute in not discussing what she felt was a private matter between her and her husband. When she refused to change her position he accused her of infidelity and at the divorce hearing he recruited his fellow ministers to attend the hearing to support him and attest to his good character.

What he didn't know was that his sexual encounter with his lover had been inadvertently recorded. She had been trying to learn how to use a new video camera she had bought and had mistakenly left it on before she left for work. When her husband's lawyer began to cross examine her about the reasons for the divorce her lawyer produced the tape for the judge and court. When the tape began playing she said she had never seen so many ministers move so swiftly in leaving a room at one time. The ministers who were willing to believe that she was a "strumpet" and a "harlot" were greeted with the sight of seeing one of their own in the throes of unprotected sexual activity with his male lover. The divorce was granted by the judge with no further deliberation necessary. However, her husband was never censored by his peers and was forgiven and given another church to pastor. One can only wonder how many of his fellow pastors were also living the secret life of the down low.

To his now former wife's credit she did not become anti-gay because of this incident. She had accepted the idea that he might stray but the hiding of his sexual preference with the probability of a greater risk of contracting HIV through unprotected sex, was more that she was willing to suffer. The aftermath of this and other experiences of abuse and neglect led her to give up trying to have relationships. She hadn't dated for more than ten years after her divorce and is very cautious when men approach her. The effects of his betrayal lingers.

The Gay Life and the Church

At another seminary I decided it was important to invite Christian members of the black gay community to my class so that my students could hear from black Christians that were gay. In attempting to discuss the role of homosexuality in the black community I invited a black lesbian and a black gay man to give a presentation to the class concerning their experiences as members of the black church and community. These were particularly enlightening and interesting classes because I also experienced the depth of the anti-gay sentiment in the black church community, not just among men, but among women as well.

When the gay male gave his talk he was greeted warmly by the black females who were concerned with the discrimination he suffered as a Christian in the churches he had attended. He related that he was not allowed to express his love for his male partners in the church and when persons discovered he was gay he was often harassed from the pulpit by the preacher making the classic remark: "God made Adam and Eve, not Adam and Steve." On more than one occasion he found himself being condemned to hell for his sexual orientation. The women were appalled by this treatment and stated that only God had the right to determine who would go to heaven or hell. They were not intimidated by his sexuality and seemed to adopt a motherly attitude toward his situation.

On the other hand the men were cold to him and one even attempted to equate homosexuality with pedophilia. In fact, I had to warn this one particular minister to stop making statements in which he said that homosexuality was the same as child abuse. It turned out to be a classic instance of projection due to guilt and shame for I later discovered that he had been incarcerated and was raped by other inmates. This experience led him to take a defensive reaction in support of his "manhood" which included a condemnation of homosexuals. His experience of sexual abuse had turned him against any expression of same sex love and led him to equate homosexuality with the most heinous sexual crime he could imagine.

After this experience I was under the mistaken notion that the black women were more accepting of homosexuality than their male peers. I thought that since they had experienced gender discrimination in the church that they were more sensitive to the plight of LGBTQ community in the church. However, when the black lesbian came to speak I discovered I was wrong. In this case the males were much more sympathetic to her situation and the females showed an obvious coldness and disgust. It became apparent that they were opposed to her sexuality because they equated it with a woman trying to be a man, something that they had been criticized for in their dealings with their churches and communities.

They were sensitive to this critique and made every effort to be as feminine as possible in order to avoid this kind of sexual stereotyping that would impede their ability to serve in the church. I have met many black female religious leaders who have also felt the necessity to hide their sexual orientation in order to avoid church censure and disapproval. The women couldn't win for losing. Whether they were gay or not they felt forced to act in a traditionally defined feminine way in order to be accepted by their churches and male peers.

This and other courses I have taught in this area has taught me how complex gender roles, sexual orientation, and sexual attitudes and behavior are among black clergy in churches and communities. The lack of an in-depth study or studies in sexuality and sexual attitudes has led to a general ignorance or confusion in the black community regarding these issues.

Instead of their theology of love informing their views on gender and sexuality, it became apparent how the black church and community's traditional adoption of gender roles and sexual attitudes dictated their actions and attitude toward women and gay persons in their community and congregations. Issues regarding homosexuality were constant features of the experiences shared by these ministers and future pastors but they had not developed an interpretation of human sexuality that was loving or ethically consistent.

Another of my female students related that when she was married she was having some difficulties with her marriage. Her husband was a Deacon in the church and that she had a difficult time making the transition from being a layperson to becoming a minister because her husband was not supportive of her goals. According to her, he became jealous of her ambitions and their marriage became more and more strained. She also suspected that he was not being faithful to her. She related that she and her husband decided to seek the counsel of their pastor. The pastor seemed concerned for their welfare and tried his best to convince her to stay with her husband. He assured her that she should trust her husband and that gradually their marriage would be healed. She accepted her pastor's counsel but one day she discovered why the pastor was so solicitous of her husband's needs.

She was suspicious regarding her husband's behavior and inadvertently came upon some information that led her to follow her husband. Upon doing so she came upon her husband and her pastor locked in a passionate embrace. This revelation left her reeling. Not only did she discover that her husband was gay, but so was her pastor. She not only felt betrayed by her husband she also felt betrayed and deceived by her pastor. She had felt that if she couldn't trust her husband she could at least trust her pastor. The pastor was the leader of one of the city's leading protestant churches. He had a wife and several children and was respected and admired by everyone in the community. Ironically, I knew the pastor's wife because at one time she was the girlfriend of one of my best friends. I had heard many years earlier that the pastor was gay but I had dismissed it as an idle rumor.

This discovery led this particular woman to leave her church and pursue ordination in another denomination. I cautioned her against developing an anti-gay attitude out of her hurt and disappointment with her pastor. I thought it was important for her to distinguish her views regarding homosexuality as distinct from the emotional betrayal she felt. I counseled her that her husband's sexuality was not the problem. Instead, it was her husband's and his pastor's dishonesty, which was in part due to their fear of retribution generated by the church and community, if their sexuality was openly known.

She was unable to take my advice and became a vocal and harsh critic of homosexuality. She separated from her husband and despite her qualifications and personal charisma she found it difficult to gain employment and expressed this frustration in class. By this time I had become familiar that some of the important actors in her profession were black and gay. I related to her that she was complaining about her gay husband and pastor to persons who were also secretly gay and if she was going to continue to work in her chosen field she would have to deal with her pain in another way. She was being viewed as someone who was scapegoating a community that was not responsible for its need to closet itself against the negative attitudes of the black church and community.

What the black community has called the down low phenomenon is very common in the black church. This is due to the total intolerance that mainstream black church leaders have maintained against same sex relationships. This complete intolerance has led pastors who are gay to hide their homosexuality by marrying and leading a hidden bisexual lifestyle. In the church they are some of the biggest anti-gay spokespersons as they extol the sanctity of marriage and denounce homosexuality as a threat to the family. However, they live a secret life in which they can indulge their sexual orientation.

Different Sexual Ethics for Men and Women

My experience working as a professor in theological seminaries was replete with these kinds of instances that emphasized the double standard of sexual conduct in the churches and community. At another seminary I was a Professor of Religion and Society where I taught courses in ethics, including a course on "Human Sexuality in the Black Community."

The class of twelve students in the sexuality course was evenly divided between black males and females. The students were members of various Protestant churches: Baptist, Methodist, Lutheran and United Church of Christ churches. About halfway through the class I joined the males at a local restaurant after class to kick it and talk informally about some of the issues that had been raised in class. Under the influence of a more relaxed atmosphere the students began to tell me about their experiences and beliefs about sexuality as they had learned and practiced these attitudes regarding sexuality from their community and spiritual leaders.

The consensus of opinion was that a man has to do what a man has to do. As males they needed sexual release and as long as the woman was willing then there was no harm. If a woman feels as though she wants to take it to a more committed relationship then it would be necessary to break things off before things got out of hand. They knew that their congregations would not fault them for their sexual dalliances as long as there were few complaints by the women involved; and there was no evidence of physical coercion or force. The marriage bond was not a barrier to outside relationships and they believed that many married women welcomed and wanted a more exciting sexual experience with their pastor.

They believed that there was a big difference between sex and love and that even then sex was still optional after marriage occurred. The first rule of sexual activity was discretion: "Don't ask, Don't tell." As long as both parties were discrete and understood the boundaries of their relationship then it was fine for the minister to enjoy the sexual bounty of his congregation. They also stated that even though they disapproved of homosexuality from the pulpit most of them said that as long as the homosexuals in the church were discrete as well, and didn't try and engage them in their sexual life, then it was live and let live. They also knew of many male ministers who were secretly gay, in what is now known as on the "Down Low". And once again as long as they were discrete, and kept to the party line of marriage fidelity, then there would be no problems in their associating with their fellow secretly gay ministers.

I was appreciative of their honesty and forthrightness while at the restaurant enjoying food and drink and expected that attitude to carry over to the classroom. The next week I raised the subject in class concerning the sexual ethics of the pastor. To my surprise every man there stated the party line. "Sex was only to occur during marriage, premarital sex was wrong, extramarital sex was wrong. The bible only allowed for heterosexual sexual activity, etc." I was shocked by this complete reversal of their previous statements. When I brought our previous conversation to their attention they were silent and refused to acknowledge the conversation. I found that the women seminarians were oblivious to the beliefs of their male counterparts. They knew that many ministers were unfaithful to their wives but they thought that it was other people's ministers and not their own. They had no idea of the pervasiveness of the male pastor's sexual ethics because most of them had not been privy to the close male mentor ship by older

male pastors as had been the case of their male classmates. These views shocked them because they were so different from the traditional views they had been raised to believe under the preaching of their male ministers growing up in the church.

It became painfully obvious to all that the traditional double standard of sexual expectations of women and men were at work. Males were expected and encouraged to defy traditional family oriented sexual ethics while the women were expected to be paragons of sexual virtue. It was important to keep up the illusion of traditional Christian ethics but another ethic was at work in the practical life of the church and community. The practical fact is that most male ministers receive their primary training in one to one or small groups of ministers who relay the traditions of their profession. Black women are seldom allowed entree in these enclaves and if they were allowed into these discussions they would probably present an obstacle to transmission of these entrenched beliefs.

My Narrative

The first time that I became aware of the abuse of pastoral authority and power was when I was a student in a theological seminary. I had several Black male friends who were also pastors and who were also studying for the ministry. I had been taught a very sexually conservative Christian understanding of sex and so I was shocked and puzzled by the libertine attitudes of my friends. It seemed as though they were in competition to see how many women they could seduce. They emphasized the number of women they could attract and seemed to be infatuated by their own appearance and pastoral gifts of preaching and teaching.

As my first marriage disintegrated my wife informed me that they had now made her the targets of their sexual attention. As their own marital relationships deteriorated they began sleeping with each other's wives in an almost competitive like atmosphere to see who was the most admired "rooster in the hen house." Instead of going into counseling to repair their marriages they substituted inappropriate sexual relationships that revealed a lack of adequate boundaries in their personal relationships.

This situation brought to mind a similar situation when I was the Chaplain and President of a Christian youth organization in my late teens and early twenties. In that case, like this one, the ministers of various churches seduced several of the young women in the youth group and also progressed to sleeping with each other's spouses.

One of the ministers started his own church by using his power to seduce the young women from the group with which I was the President. In his attempt to build a church of his own he used an extremely patriarchal interpretation of the Bible to justify his sexual abuse of power. Psychologically, he used his status as a father figure to seduce these young women who were starved for male attention and affection. This minister, as in the previous example, began to engage in sexual activity with other spouses. They justified their activity as sanctioned by the Bible's giving authority to men to fulfill their sexual needs. Their sexual proclivities, which seemed to know no bounds, resulted in the psychological destruction of many of the young women with whom they had affairs. As I reflect on this experience I realize that there was not only an issue of boundary maintenance, but the leader of the group also had a perverse understanding of sexuality which fueled his desire to humiliate his wife and women in general.

In both situations there was a sense of normality concerning their behavior. They were even able to quote scriptures that they said provided justification for their actions. These activities occurred close to the time of Jim Jones' destruction of his Jonestown congregation in Guyana which featured much of these same hyper patriarchal views of sexuality and sexual abuse. Jones himself had been taught by Black religious leaders who had perfected their "game" concerning the exploitation of women.

In my initial days as a professing Christian I had realized that a close reading of the Bible was of little help in developing a consistent sexual ethic. Religious leaders who professed to be Bible believing Christians had no consistent ethic regarding issues concerning divorce; extra and pre-marital sex; sexual practices; and the like. Those that professed a conservative evangelical ethic, more often than not, were living a different sexual ethic in their private lives. When I became a minister and seminary professor I was careful to follow the ethical guidelines of the churches, seminaries and universities. However, it was a struggle to maintain appropriate boundaries since the ethical norms in the black church were either undefined or inconsistent with traditional norms.

It wasn't until one of my married female advisees told me about an affair she had with another professor that I began to question my actions and those of my peers. She stated that she had fallen in love with her professor and that she had informed her husband of their affair. This led to a marital crisis involving the possible break up of her family in which there were children involved. The professor, who had no intention of having a serious relationship with her, also found that his marriage and career were in jeopardy since this was not the first time that a student had complained of his sexual misconduct. I was heartbroken to see the pain she was suffering and I realized that there is a thin line between mutual consent and the abuse of power. In situations of power imbalance it is rare that harm does not occur to the less powerful subject, the institution and often to the more powerful person in the relationship.

Does this mean that I believe that professors and students; and pastors and their members should never engage in mutually agreed upon romantic liaisons? Yes and No. Yes, in that I believe in the right of persons to find love in varied work situations as long as it is clear that the person with less power will not be harmed. This means informing appropriate officials of the relationship and insuring that if the relationship goes sour the person with the least power will not be harmed. There must be transparency so that the more powerful person cannot engage in or be accused of favoritism toward his/her lover. Many persons find their soul mates and future partners at the work site but the guidelines as to whether and in what form relationships will be allowed must be clear.

No, in that I believe that the spiritual and psychological dynamics between a pastor and his congregation; and often a teacher and student, are too laden with emotional dependency to provide a basis for a loving and just relationship. There may be exceptions, but this only proves the rule. Should relationships between clergy and parishioners take place? My answer is never. The only possible exception would be if both persons were unmarried and had undergone extensive counseling before entering into the relationship. It is too easy to mistake feelings of dependency and transference that can mislead clergy and lay persons to engage in romances that are ill fated and morally questionable.

The media circus regarding the allegations against Bishop Eddie Long once again brought this issue of the pastoral abuse of authority to the forefront of the black and national community. Bishop Long was accused by several young men in his congregation of an abuse of pastoral authority. He is alleged to have seduced these young men who were members of his church and young men's fellowship into participating in various sexual activities when they were sixteen years old. The case was later settled out of court and will remain unexamined and inconclusive. The state of Georgia has declined to prosecute because these young men had reached the age of maturity and were not considered minors. Therefore, from a criminal legal point of view Long may be innocent. The important question that this situation points to is the issue of the pastoral abuse of power and how the black church understands abuse of power. This had to do with the back church and community's interpretation of the function of sexuality and its use and abuse in both a moral and professional sense.

In addition to the issue of abuse of power the issue of homosexuality and gay rights has also become an issue. Long had developed a high public profile reputation for being anti-gay and opposed to same sex marriage. Many persons in the black community who support his views have been vocal defenders of Rev. Long. Many, if not most of his church members still support him even though he has not gone on record in categorically denying that he engaged in sexual activity with his young parishioners.

Long has had many defenders in his church and from other black churches and members. This situation begs the question as to why the black community is so divided over these issues and what are the ways in which both Long's detractors and supporters understand sexuality and the abuse of power. Because there has been such a silence regarding the issue of sexuality in the black churches and community it is virtually left rudderless to define how it determines what are the ethical and moral ways that sexuality should be expressed. The confusion over the rightness or wrongness of the alleged actions of Rev. Long are the symptoms of a much deeper ethical situation.

The abuse of pastoral power has been a long standing problem in the black church community. Accusations against black pastors abusing their power are common place but they have seldom been addressed. The history and social context of the black churches have placed them in a unique place regarding issues of sexuality and sexual ethics. The result is that there have been little disciplined consideration of the ethical nature of sexuality and pastoral abuse of power from the black church community.

When sexuality has been discussed by black church theologians, ministers and ethicists they have dealt with the issue by simply restating traditional Christian views that outlaw any sexual behavior outside of traditional marriage. Some have been bold enough to discuss sexuality but even this discussion has been primarily around issues of the place of homosexuality and even then on a limited scale. In some ways this is like putting the cart before the horse. It is difficult to deal with ethical issues when there is little agreement on the norms by which you are judging behaviors that may fall outside the norm. Even less has been written about the abuse of power by black clergy.

My experience with religious denominational publishers is that they also have avoided this topic. The reason may be as simple as a wish to avoid conflict or reprisal by prominent black religious leaders, an ignorance of the importance of the subject or because they recognize that this issue is so widespread in the black churches that fear the possibility that black religious leaders would should be protected against these kinds of inquiry. There may also be the fear that any interrogation into this topic may be misunderstood as "airing dirty laundry" and should be kept within the auspices of the black churches and community, lest the black community be demonized by the general public as tales of sexual misconduct become common knowledge. Now that the story of Bishop Long has been well publicized the black churches and black community are ready to engage in a serious discussion of these issues.

The socializing that occurs among black pastors is meant to initiate younger ministers into the ideas that men in power and authority, especially black pastors, should not be held accountable to the same standards of conduct that exist for other professionals who are charged with the mental and physical health of those whom they serve. The biggest battle is to develop awareness of the problem and that is in fact a problem. After this is acknowledged it is possible to develop relationships that are just, caring and devoid of exploitation.

My own experiences with the black church allowed me to gain a first-hand experience of the sexual misconduct that routinely occurs. I could have written about many other incidents that were just as egregious as those mentioned in this text but it would have been impossible to disguise the identities of the persons who were involved in those incidents. I hope that by giving these snapshots of the effects of sexual misconduct the reader will gain an inkling of the widespread and serious nature of the problem.

I have been teaching and writing about this topic for over twenty years. An earlier book: <u>Black Sexual Ethics: The Uses and Misuses of Sexuality</u> was a self-published attempt to deal with this topic since traditional religious presses found it too controversial to publish. This book is now out of print and to some extent my views have changed in a way that I hope have become more precise in interpreting this phenomenon in the black church community. The next chapter will deal more directly with the reasons why many black pastors abuse their authority.

African American Sexual Ethics: Between the Spirituals and the Blues

Every time I Feel the Spirit Moving in My Heart I will Pray
Traditional African American Spiritual
My Lord, What Did I Do to be So Black and Blue
Traditional African American Blues

Maintaining Improper Boundaries: Black Folk Ethic of Pastoral Abuse

I mentioned that I black male ministers are introduced to an ethical framework that allowed black clergy to engage in sexual relationships with their members. In one of these informal "teaching sessions" I was at a meeting with a well-known and respected clergy person with a group of aspiring young black male ministers and theologians. "Dr. Charisma" as, I will call him, was known as one of the most successful and innovative pastors in the black community. After an initial discussion on how he became a successful pastor he began to explain why so many of his church members were female and why he was known to have been sexually involved with several of these women.

He explained that ideas of sexuality were different in the black community as compared to the traditional Christian views espoused by the predominantly white community. I had already heard from several women who had been involved with Dr. Charisma and so I carefully listened to his explanation. These women genuinely admired their pastor and did not want to be responsible for "bringing down a black man" that had done so much for them and other members of the community. Dr. Charisma explained that the puritanical sexual view of the white churches and pastors were due to their uncritical, and in many cases, their limited understanding of biblical scripture. He felt as though traditional Christian sexual attitudes were unnecessarily restrictive.

This was not to be the only justification I would hear from black clergy as to why it was appropriate to engage in extra-marital relationships. Another well-known pastor had developed a philosophy in which he asserted that it was the Christian duty of female members to provide sexual services to their spiritual leaders. He called this philosophy the missionary "f--k." Unfortunately, many African American pastors affirmed his philosophy although it may have a different nomenclature, or not named as well. I have found that many church women have assented to this perspective and will defend their pastor's actions as long as some modicum of discretion is involved. It seems that many Black church persons are so accustomed to accepting the misconduct of their pastors that it is now assented to as normal behavior. In effect, because their moral compass has never been set to understand the dynamics and damaging effects of pastoral sexual misconduct they have developed a kind of denial regarding their minister's sexual misconduct. I doubt whether most or even many black church persons have any idea of what it means for a pastor to engage in acts of abuse of power. The typical Black pastor commands and expects such love and devotion that it has almost become expected that he will abuse his power and be forgiven for it.

Like many black pastors Dr. Charisma also believed that monogamy, like homosexuality, was a white thing and that the black community need not be influenced by these notions. In other words being Black and heterosexual became an excuse for sexual misconduct. In the same way that homosexuality was claimed to be "a white thing," sexual fidelity was also seen as a feature of white ethic and spirituality. In their understanding of human sexuality, male leaders deserved sexual privileges and also were not expected to control their sexual desires. Therefore they should be excused when they attempt to satisfy their sexual desires with various females in the congregation since that is their divinely appointed privilege just as it is the woman's role to sexually service their pastor.

This unwillingness to criticize the pastor is indicative of the blind trust and devotion that a community under crisis has given its spiritual leaders. Ultimately, this devotion has also resulted in a lack of ability for churches to cooperate with each other as each church and its leader developed a social and sexual fiefdom of its own. Each church requires a single minded devotion to their particular pastor and leader and is therefore willing to overlook the misconduct of its leaders and has a limited capacity to trust other churches and their leaders.

Eventually Dr. Charisma was brought up on charges by some of these women to denominational officials but since this was a church of immense influence nothing was ever done to deal with the situation. This was unfortunate for the women who had been the victims of his misconduct and for the pastor as well; for it diminished their capacity to develop healthier ways of relating; and it gave the pastor an air of invincibility regarding his activities, which only led to more misconduct and complaints in the future.

Self-Deception-Discretion-Silence

In addition to the narratives given in the previous chapters I have almost never met an African American person who was not aware of sexual misconduct in their churches even if they did not name it as such. Another senior black church official told me of a minster under his care who was involved in multiple sexual relationships in the congregation. His behavior was brought to the pastor's attention by several of the older women in the church. They complained about his behavior, but not for the purpose of him not dating within the church. Instead, they were displeased because he had not made a clear choice in terms of whom he wanted to marry. They saw his behavior as disrespectful of the marital aspirations of the several women with whom he was actively dating. This minister had transgressed this boundary with his many sexual partners and so the older church women informed the senior minister that the assistant pastor would have to make a choice and therefore not play with the affections of his female partners. It was a case of harming the women who had hopes of finding a husband, and it was also a case of violating the boundary of a sexual ethic of discretion which was meant to avoid disharmony and conflict within the congregation.

The women were not setting the boundary forbidding sexual contact between the minister and the congregation. However, the minister had violated the sexual ethic of discretion, which has to do with the sexual practices of persons kept private and hidden from the larger social group. In this view the value is to "mind one's business." Since sexuality is a taboo topic, the reasons for which will be discussed more fully, discussion of one's own sexuality is placed behind a veil of secrecy and privacy. This means that discussion of sexuality is removed from public discussion and becomes primarily a private affair. Its regulation is solely the province of the individuals involved.

The self-deception that has occurred within the ministerial community can almost defy description and belief. One well known senior minister in a large urban church was called upon to support one of his junior ministers who had been charged by an unmarried female parishioner with sexual misconduct. The parishioner asserted that though the minister was married he had seduced her and fathered her child. The minister vehemently denied the charges. The senior minister gathered support for his younger charge from other parishioners and ministers and charged the woman with being immoral, a liar and manipulative. This senior minister was present at the church hearing where this case was being heard when the DNA results were opened and read. The charged minister, to the chagrin of the senior minister and his associates, was indeed found to be the father of the child. This led to the junior minister being placed under probation and adequate compensation made to the woman who had suffered the deception of the minister, the vilification by the Senior Pastor as well as the disdain of other ministers and members of the church community.

This atmosphere of hostility by church officials toward women who speak out against their abusers has had a chilling effect on the willingness of abused women and men to speak out against those pastors who have abused their authority. This is compounded by the silence of women and men who are aware of their pastor's activities but choose to allow them to engage in activities that are injurious to black women, children and families. I mention the women specifically at this point because the Black Church's membership is anywhere from 70-80% female. More men may be in authority as ministers but it is women who hold the power of the purse and service. They are the stewards of the church and should make clear to their leaders that they expect loving and professional behavior in their spiritual leaders.

The fact that most black churches are primarily composed of women has intensified this issue and often the pastor finds himself the object of competition by various women in the church. In a community where the number of suitable male partners is pathetically low due to unemployment and lack of education, this intensifies the desire to see the pastor as an emotional and sexual partner and may serve to heighten feelings of transference and counter transference.

Churches and religious bodies should be clear concerning their policies in this area and develop clear policies and strong sanctions regarding a violation of their rules. Just as in college teaching where some colleges prohibit any sexual contact between professors and students; others may allow it but with very clear rules regarding the relationship being acknowledged and reported, and the professor not being allowed to be in a position of power over the student. This protects the rights of the student and professor since any relationship can become toxic. There are many ways to approach boundary setting but each religious body should be clear and open about their rules and expectations for their clergy. Any sexual contact between clergy and minors should be prohibited and appropriate rules and procedures regarding clergy contact with minors should be in place. This includes background screening of clergy conduct for complaints regarding sexual misconduct. Sexual abuse is an abuse of Power by the powerful minister against the less powerful parishioner and should be understood and treated as such.

The previous examples reveal the difficulty that Black pastors have in maintaining appropriate emotional boundaries. It is important to continue this analysis by examining the cultural situation that helped produce these attitudes and behaviors and, in the next chapter, examining the two most prominent African American religious leaders of contemporary times in order to provide more evidence and depth to this analysis.

Historical and Cultural Factors in the Sexual Abuse of Power in the Black Church:
"Rapetalism"

The thesis of this book is that the sexual abuse of power by African American male clergy is pervasive within the black community. It is the claim of this chapter that this practice is acknowledged within the African American churches and that it is justified by the development of an ethical discourse that has been the result of the historical-social context that is particular to the Black community. This social context, which I have termed rapetalism: the combination and confluence of a history of racial, sexual and economic oppression, has been the always already dialogue partner for the development of this silencing ideological discourse which has allowed sexual misconduct to have free reign in African American churches. This discourse hides the presence of the underlying psychological and ethical issues that gave rise and help to perpetuate this abuse of power. It is my contention that the Black Church and Black community's ethical discourse has been in reaction to this oppressive social context and has not been able to develop a liberating ethical discourse that can constrain the presence of sexual abuse. ***To put it plainly, it is impossible to prevent sexual abuse if it is not recognized as abuse.***

The perspective of this chapter is that the previously victimized Black community has now adopted the Rapetalistic sexual discourse of their oppressors. The Black church has institutionalized the oppressive patriarchal position of their historical perpetrators. The transition from the legal polygamy of Africa, into the "illegal polygamy" as described by Du Bois in the The Soul of Black Folks, has become the dominant sexual discourse that promotes this abuse of power. It is analogous to the battered wife and child syndrome writ large in which the victim comes to identify with his/her oppressor. The image of the black preacher as father, lover and protector only serves to reinforce a patriarchal social process in which both the victim (community and church) and the victimizer (leadership) have become unwitting partners in the continuation of sexually abusive practices.

The following chart proposes a historical overview of the development of this sexual ethical discourse. It will be followed by a further analysis of the implication of this ethical framework.

*Chart-A Historical Overview of African American Sexual Ethics * see Appendix*

The Spirituals and the Blues

Sexual ethics in the African American community can best be described by referring to the Spirituals and Blues. The Spirituals represents what I call the Sexual Ethics of Discretion. This ethic involves an emphasis on building strong traditional families according to traditional Euro-American Christian values. In the African American community it includes a silence on sexual matters due to issues of personal privacy and cultural safety. The Blues sexual ethics, which I term an Ethics of Pleasure, emphasizes an orientation toward an appreciation of the erotic aspects of sexual activity which may take socially illicit forms.

Both of these sexual ethics have cultural forces which promote their ascendancy in the African American community. The church, the media, the entertainment industry all has effects on the sexual values and mores of African Americans. The church, obviously, tends to promote the Spiritual sexual ethic, while the media and the entertainment industry have tended to promote the Blues ethic. This does not mean that African Americans participate exclusively in one or the other sexual ethic. In fact there is significant interchange between the two ethical orientations. It has almost become a cliche that most popular rhythm and blues artists got their start in the church singing the spirituals and gospel music. Just as there has been mutual participation in both musical spheres, the same can be said of the interchange of sexual ethical orientations. This has resulted in more than a little confusion among the African American community itself about the nature of appropriate sexual ethics.

Apollonian and Dionysian Ethical Perspectives

The great German philosopher, Frederic Nietzsche, created similar categories in his first book, "The Birth of Tragedy," in which he defined the predominant perspectives that marked ancient Greek culture. He wrote about two perspectives: the Apollonian spirit which featured the rational and orderly, vs. the Dionysian spirit which was chiefly the world of the ecstatic and wild. The African American community has also operated out of a dualism:

The Spirituals and The Blues.

The originator of African American Theology James Cone, first wrote about these perspectives in ways that have not been fully appreciated or challenged by his colleagues. However, I believe that it is the power of this dualism that has prevented the development of a sexual ethic that most African Americans can recognize and accept. For Nietzsche, Christianity represented the development of an Apollonian moral perspective that squashed the joy and vigor of life. Its views on the renunciation of the world of sensuality was the full culmination of an Apollonian spirit that was made manifest in the Socratic dialogues. In contrast to this perspective Traditional African culture had an emphasis on ecstasy and spirited worship in which movement of the body was a part of worship. African culture was not without rules regarding sexuality but compared to European Christianity it valued the body and understood human sexuality and sexual desire as a necessary and non-sinful part of human existence. Sexuality and sexual feelings were not repressed but like religious feelings they could be felt and expressed within the norms of their society.

Just as these two perspectives represented different views of love and faith, like the spirituals and the blues, they also share some of the same features. It must be remembered that not only did the Apollonian perspective represent rationality for the Greeks; the famous Oracle of Delphi was a follower of Apollo. Yet, her non-rational prophetic utterances were carried out within the institutionalized and hierarchical social order. WEB Du Bois likens the trance like ecstatic state of the Delphic Oracle to the frenzy of African American folks' expression of their Spirituals in his classic work; "The Souls of African American Folk." The Spirituals, like the Delphic Oracle, represented the official religion as it emphasized a rational approach as it relied on Scripture but it was not long before the more conservative representatives of evangelical Christianity attempted to suppress the ecstatic nature of

African American religion and sought to ban the singing of Spirituals due to the possibility that they would be sung with too much emotion.

Just as the Apollonian was to suppress the Dionysian style of worship and being in the world; the leaders of the African American churches sought respectability by developing a spiritual form of worship without the excess of emotion. However this ecstatic experience took shape in the form of the Blues, as a spiritual style which affirmed the body, sexuality and the non-rational and included a place for the full expression of the emotional life that had been suppressed by evangelical religion. Pentecostalism, which originated during this same time frame, was an attempt to include both non-rational and the conservative ethical doctrines that the Blues ignored. Neither the Blues nor Pentecostalism found favor in mainstream African American churches and so this inability to effectively define a consistent religious and ethical perspective led to a general sense of confusion about religious and ethical issues in the African American community.

Would and should the sexual ethics represented by a conservative view of religion prevail? Or should a sexual ethic of the Blues in which sensuality and an acceptance of the body hold sway? What happened was an amalgam of both views which left both perspectives wanting in clarity and consistency. Dionysus was the Greek god who brought wine to the common people who needed a way to escape the enforced drudgery and order of a strict Patriarchal world. Similarly, the Blues performers and participants filled the same function, and like the followers of Dionysus were known for the participation of females who celebrated their unique sexual and sensual powers. Like the Dionysian world of excess the Blues ethos created a space for an acceptance of the world of spirited expression that did not conform to expected notions of public order. African American community members were forced by the Spiritual community to choose between the Orderly God's (Apollonian) music and way of life (Hymns, Anthems, Spirituals, Gospel) or the Non-rational (Dionysian) Devil's music and way of life (The Blues). The Dionysian ethos of the Blues with its inclusion of an African religious style was opposed by an Evangelical Christianity, which could not include aspects of the rational and orderly with the sensual and celebrative.

In private however there was often a mixing of these two spiritual styles in the African American community so that religious officials may have preached against the Blues on Sunday but went to hear he Blues on Saturday or on the radio on Monday. This intermingling of these two spiritual styles made the development of a consistent sexual ethic problematic. For in truth, the African American community did not want to give up either perspective. Its members recognized the value of each perspective. In a true conformity to an African understanding of religion in which both are valuable parts of the whole African American leaders found themselves between a rock and a hard place as they tried to live between the Spirituals and the Blues.

For instance, The Spirituals and the Blues are both sensual music which involve the use of the body. The African American Ring Shout in Slave Christianity featured the movement of the body in worship. This has transferred in the historical and contemporary modes of religious expression in the African American community. The lively processionals of gospel choirs and the clapping, dancing and other rhythmic movement of African Americans under the influence of spiritual ecstasy are testimony to the persistent power of the Dionysian revelry within African American religious expression. In the African American churches the rational needs of beliefs in doctrines and strict Christian moral values are blended with the emotional fervor of a danced religion.

The Blues also share this mixed message but not to the same extent since it was a music that did not need nor seek social approval from the larger society. The blues were born in the work gangs and in dance halls and juke joints. African American folks burdened down by life's troubles sought spiritual and emotional fulfillment through song and dance that was not only sensual but overtly sexual as well. This Dionysian revelry was not only practiced and enjoyed by those outside of the church but many Christian faithful also enjoyed the vitality of the blues. The open secret that you might see your church leader on Saturday at the Juke Joint and in the front row of the Church on Sunday became a common observation. Although there were many who still subscribed to a complete separation of God's music: The Spirituals and Gospel music vs. the Devil's music. In reality this total separation was not possible for even Gospel music itself was borne from the chord structure and inspiration of repentant blues musicians. It was not uncommon for the worst sinner and singer of the Blues to include a spiritual or gospel song on their record albums and musical acts.

African American churches wanted and admired leaders who had been educated and influenced theologically by the Apollonian like nature of a Christianity that separated the rational from the body but at the same time the African American churches valued their religious leaders that could combine and inculcate these two perspectives. They wanted ministers who were educated in the theology of evangelical Christianity but who were also sensual and sexual in their style of ministry and preaching. They did not want imitators of white Christianity to lead them but they also wanted the down to earth nature of leaders who understood why African American folks got the blues. This attempt to have one's cake and eat it too was done without a cultural space to discuss the ramifications of these two perspectives.

This internal contradiction set the stage for the present situation in which African American religious leaders and lay-persons have a great deal of difficulty in defining a sexual ethic that is true to the sensual and the spiritual. The movement from a Traditional African sexual ethic which included both the sensual and the spiritual; to the sexual ethic during slavery which was based on a dualism in which Blacks struggled to overcome their exploitation by emphasizing discretion and order; to the Blues ethic in which psychological hedonism and ethical egoism reigned has left the Black Church and community ethically adrift and floundering on the shores of America's landscape. (See chart in Appendix)

The task of the Black theological and ethical community is to reconstruct or construct a sexual ehtic that is true to the goals of love and justice in interpersonal social relationships. It will not be an easy or simple task.

Summary and Discussion

The current controversy regarding sexual misconduct whether it be the alleged or actual actions of Herman Cain, Bishop Eddie Long, Coach Sandusky of Penn State, Fitzpatrick of the Boston Red Sox, Clarence Thomas, Jesse Jackson, Jesse Jackson Jr., Michael Jackson, Mike Tyson, Martin Luther King, Jr., Bill Cosby, Booker T. Washington, W.E.B. Du Bois, our first "black" president; Bill Clinton, etc. points to the reality of the pervasive presence of a failure of the black community to develop an ethical and psychological discourse that can prevent the abuse of power in the black community. These present allegations are the tip of an ethical iceberg that is taking a severe toll on the well-being of the black family and churches in America.

When the traditional leaders have adopted an oppressive ideology what hope do the masses have? Is it any wonder that black males are the least and the last to develop committed relationships? There is a lack of care towards black women in the church due to the patriarchal ideology that has supported the exploitation of black women in the church. I believe that another factor that is seldom mentioned is the probability that many black pastors have been the victims of childhood sexual abuse as well. There is an atmosphere of the over sexualization of black boys and men which also contributes to this issue that I cannot address in this paper. The recent revelations of the experience of sexual abuse by luminous personalities like Tyler Perry and the continued surfacing of victims in the Penn State case will keep this issue in the forefront. This issue challenges notions of black masculinity in ways that will require further in-depth treatment at a later date.

Should it surprise any of us when we hear of the continued sexual exploitation of black boys and girls in a community that has hidden its own shadow side from itself as it sought to hide its sexual activities from the gaze of the critical eyes of the hypocritical white church? What is needed is an open dialogue about sexual ethics in the black community. Even the current concern over homosexuality in the black church ignores the long standing exploitive patriarchal ideology that supports the exploitation of black women and children as well as its black gay community.

The sexual taboo that silences the black community from discussing sex in general has also led to a silencing of the presence and extent of the sexual abuse of power in the black church. As a survivor of childhood sexual abuse I feel the pain of my sisters and brothers who have suffered and are suffering due to this failure to develop an even relatively adequate psycho-ethical understanding of sexual practices and abuse in the black community. Hopefully, we will not let this issue pass and the church will begin to address the deep seated ethos and ethics which allows this abuse to continue.

Chapter Three

The Sexual Ethics of Malcolm and Martin

The lives of Malcolm X and Martin Luther King, Jr. can help serve as examples of African American Sexual Ethics. Not only are these two of the most influential figures in contemporary African American history; their lives have been made open to the public by numerous biographies and articles. Therefore it is possible to have a common starting point in a conversation which considers the abuse of power as it pertains to religious leaders among African American clergy. in addition their sexual attitudes, actions and ethics have been the subject of controversy and continued concern for the last forty years. The recent biography by Manning Marable (Malcolm X: A Life of Reinvention) has stoked the fires of controversy regarding the sexual ethics of Malcolm X. as detractors and supporters of Marable's work have attempted to discover the "real" sexual attitudes and practices of this African American icon.

By examining these two African Americans' sexual attitudes and practices I hope to reveal how the previous discussion can help us to interpret the sexual ethics that exist within the African American community. Their narratives can serve as ideal types in the construction and deconstruction of African American sexual discourse as we see the lived sexual ethics of these African American religious leaders who were the product and subsequent role-models for generations of African American religious leadership.

Martin Luther King, Jr.

Sexuality was an important part of Martin Luther King Jr.'s life. If the colloquialism is true that a person's spirituality is reflected by their sexuality, then this was certainly true of Dr. King's sexual life. His sexual drive was certainly reflected and intrinsic in terms of his charismatic attraction. An examination of his prolific sexual behavior gives credence to the idea that sexual charisma and charismatic leadership are related. King's sexual life became an issue for the public when biographers revealed that the FBI had attempted to blackmail Dr. King into renouncing his leadership position by making public his extramarital affairs. King had incurred the wrath of then FBI Director, J. Edgar Hoover, who suspected King of being a communist sympathizer. During surveillance of Dr. King the FBI learned of King's many sexual liaisons and sent a tape recording of Dr. King's sexual activities to his home. This was done in order to embarrass the Civil Rights leader into submission and serve as a warning that the FBI could expose him at any moment.

However, this did not prevent King from continuing his leadership role in the Civil Rights struggle. Accounts of this incident reveal that his wife Coretta did not berate him for his actions. When the information became public after King's death I remember listening to a radio broadcast of Operation Push in Chicago, Illinois in which Rev. Jesse Jackson, one of King's inner circle, made light of these findings by repeatedly shouting in the microphone "so what?". In this statement, Jackson echoed the sentiments of many African American community members who took a view that a person's sexual life is a private matter and should not be a major factor in the ways by which we judge our spiritual leaders. I have termed this position as The Spiritual Ethic of Discretion. This sexual hedonism and ethical egoism has been a part of what has made it so difficult for the African American Church to establish norms concerning sexual misconduct and abuse.

King's biographers have reported that King did not take his actions lightly. Apparently, his attitudes toward his exposure as an adulterer resulted in great mental pain and anguish. His biographers and the messages found in his later sermons gives a picture of a man full of self-recrimination and doubt concerning his inability to remain faithful to his wife. No biographer reports that King ever attempted to justify his actions on moral or any other grounds. His wife, Coretta Scott King was also silent about his moral inconsistency. Like most men of his time he joked about his sexual exploits with his companions who were also aware of his sexual activities before he realized that the FBI was recording his activities. Whether his later anguish and regret were due to the embarrassment it would cause him and his movement; or was sincere and real moral regret is left only for Dr. King to answer. We have no record by those who participated in his sexual life to further determine his attitudes toward his own sexual conduct.

Dr. King was trained in ethics and in his sermons he is very clear about the necessity to be faithful within the bounds of matrimony. Once again; whether he had a sense of remorse concerning his own unfaithfulness to his wife Coretta, or saw himself as a part of a larger tradition we cannot at present know due to a lack of evidence. Perhaps those conversations have not yet been released by his archivists. What can be said is that Dr. King is emblematic of many African American preachers who have felt compelled to preach an ethic they either did not believe in and/or could not fulfill in their personal lives. The maxim: "practice what you preach," has led to serious doubters within the African American community regarding the ethical leadership of black pastors. The truthfulness and sincerity of African American preachers who advocate traditional Christian family values but live another ethical lifestyle has been a criticsm and question that the black community has carried for many years. This is what I have called living between The Spirituals and The Blues. This apparent double standard and confusion regarding sexual ethics represents the result of the silencing of the discussion regarding sexuality and the distortion of sexuality in the African American church and community.

We also have to wonder whether Dr. King's relationships with women revealed a patriarchal attitude toward women that is deep seated in African American clergy. While Dr. King's male lieutenants like Ralph Abernathy, Jesse Jackson and Andrew Young, among others, became well known public figures, the women who were closely associated with King did not receive the same adulation and status as their male counterparts. Is it probably safe to state that King had a difficult time in viewing women as equals. Instead, women were viewed in more traditional patriarchal African and Christian Euro-American ways which emphasized their second hand status and objectification as sexual objects.

The role of African American women in the Civil Rights Movement has been a point of contention by many African American scholars and feminists. These scholars tend to view the Civil Rights movement as an attempt by African American males to gain power while African American women were their main soldiers and supporters. Instead of exercizing leadership black women were expected to remain in secondary roles. Unfortunately, we have little direct knowledge of how Dr. King felt about women's rights since the Civil Rights movement as the main vehicle for the rights of the black community in general was the main focus of his speeches, sermons and activities. However this may be a case of when silence speaks volumes. Surely King was aware of the centuries old struggle for womwn's equality. As a Boston trained social ethicist his quietism regarding the rights of women is suspiciously absent and may give further credence to a chauvanistic view of King. Just as it took King a while to get on board the anti-war train we may have reason to hope that he may have also changed his more traditional views concerning the role of women. His ability to accept and embrace the presence, advice and companionship of the openly Gay Civil Rights activist; Bayard

Rustin may speak for the possibility for his capacity for change on issues of sexuality and gender roles.

This is all conjecture of course since there seems to be little to suggest that King went outside the norm of middle class gentility in his public persona and family situation. His sexual proclivities meet the expectations of what I term the African American community's sexual ethics of discretion, and although he showed remorse after his sexual secrets were discovered he apparently made no vows to reform his actions. He may have simply recognized his sexual activity as a moral weakness; "a thorn in the flesh" that he had to bear. But this is speculation since we do not yet have access to King's written or spoken insights to inform us on this matter.

Malcolm X

It is beneficial for our purposes to contrast King's sexual ethics to that of Malcolm X, his nemesis and rival in life and in death. Like Dr. King, the life of Malcolm X reveals a particular patterning and ideology of sexual ethics in the African American community. The life of Malcolm X is a ringing testimony to the power of human sexuality and its particular expressions in the African American community. Malcolm X as moral reprobate and moral reformer reveals the flip sides of sexuality in the African American community. The early part of Malcolm's sexual ethics is reminiscent of The Blues Sexual Ethic in which the experience of pleasure was the major goal. As Malcolm's life is known through The Autobiography by Alex Haley his early sexual life was dominated by a hedonist and egoistic ethical philosophy. While much of what Haley has written has undergone challenge, including whether Haley's account should have included material considering whether Malcolm engaged in homosexual activities as a youth, Haley's biography still stands as the most authoritative document of Malcolm's life.

Malcolm's life from his birth to his death shows the central role of sexuality as it was lived out for many black males in the social experience of rapetalistic oppression. Malcolm's life journey reveals how the interaction of racial, class and sexual oppression are central to the construction of identity in the African American community. His father was a dark complexioned African American man who married a light skinned woman. Only under the social specter of slavery and racial segregation and discrimination does it take on a heightened importance as a social marker. It was, and to some extent, still is an especially important social marker since in the United States, the lighter the back person was the more access to social goods and privileges (see Obama).

His lighter skin color, due to his being the biological product of a mother whose family was more light skinned tone and his darkly complexioned father intensified the issue of rapetalistic oppression. This situation was further intensified for Malcolm since his father was a proponent of Marcus Garvey's Black Nationalist movement in which the African American aphorism; "the blacker the berry the sweeter the juice" was a key part of a philosophy of black pride. This belief was contra the African American aphorism of; "If you're black get back, if you're brown stick around, if you're white you're right. From a Garveyite perspective in which blacker skin color was thought to be more aesthically pleasing the ideas of white supremacy were resisted on the aesthetic level. The desirability of African physical features was championed by Garvey and his legions of followers, including his father.

Therefore, Malcolm's mother was apologetic about her skin color and Malcolm learned to hate the "redness" of his skin as evidence of the sexual violation of his ancestors under slavery. Malcolm would often regale his listeners with stories of the sexual violence perpetrated by white males against African American females. A subject of which he freely spoke during his tenure as a Muslim minister.

I once asked one of my seminary classes whether they felt that skin color was still important in the African American community when it came to male-female relationships. This particular class had a preponderance of light skinned African American women, and much to my surprise they were very forceful in stating that African American males treated them like sexual objects because of their skin color. In fact, they stated that they felt as though they were treated more like sexual objects than their darker skinned sisters.

They also spoke about how they had to deal with these issues with their children and other African American young people who were also dealing with these issues. One woman spoke about her daughter who wished that her features were more traditionally African in this day of Afro=centrism and African American pride. This may still be more of a factor in the African American community than the community wishes to acknowledge since much of African American leadership still tends to lean toward lighter featured African American persons. Light skinned African American men and women may still have an advantage in obtaining sexual and marital partners as African Americans still seek to fulfill the expectations of the color bar. I was surprised when one woman told me that many of her inner-city teenaged companions were engaging in genetic engineering. When I asked her what she meant by that statement; she stated that many of her girlfriends were choosing light skinned African American males to impregnate them so that their offspring would be as light skinned as possible.

Malcolm believed that the fear of African American-white sexuality was an important factor in the construction of America. He believed that he received such a harsh sentence for his participation in a burglary ring because he was sexually involved with the white woman partner he recruited into his ring. As he put it, he believed and stated that he was convicted for sleeping with a white woman, rather than for his activity as a burglar.

Some writers have speculated on the possibility that Malcolm may have been gay or bisexual during his younger years. However the refusal to entertain this possibility and the controversy generated by this speculation may speak more about the anti-gay stance of many within the African American community than it does concerning Malcolm's sexuality. This is true of the traditional African American churches and African American cultural nationalist groups that believe that homosexuality is a sinful, or "immoral European" practice. They assert that African Americans who engage in same sex relationships have been led astray by a sexually deviant white community..

Like King, Malcolm himself does not mention his view of homosexuality or his sexual orientation. He does claim to have practiced most "sins", before his conversion to Islam under the Honorable Elijah Muhammad, but whether this included homosexual activity is not known. Malcolm is clear that he engaged in sexual activity with single and married women alike without impunity during his early years as a street hustler. His reckless sexual activity included liaisons with white women and he describes his African American partner in crime as having a sexual fixation with white women. This is a scenario that has been attested to by many African American males; Eldridge Cleaver being the most infamous. According to The Autobiography, Malcolm's relationship with his white female in crime was to be Malcolm's last sexual foray with women, including white women, outside the boundary of marriage.

After his release from prison he developed a philosophy concerning women that combined his own experiences and that of the teaching of his newly found spiritual leader; Elijah Muhammad. As was consistent with traditional patriarchal religious belief, this philosophy stated that women were the natural inferiors of men, bearers of sin, and should be protected as befits the strong (the Male) protecting the weak (the Female). Malcolm had also developed a deep mistrust of women during his years as a street hustler and these experiences played into Elijah's negative views of women.

According to Elijah, Muslim men were expected to be the heads of their household and manage their wife and children in traditional patriarchal fashion. Malcolm also reported Elijah Muhammad's teachings about the correct age that women and men should marry; half the man's age plus seven. Malcolm had an extremely negative attitude toward women and constantly warned his fellow Muslim brothers not to be caught unaware by scheming women. It was not until Malcolm's world travels and his conversion to Sunni Islam did he break with a paternalistic image of women. He repeatedly called for the "progressive" position in which women should receive the same economic and educational benefits as males. He believed that the progress of any society could be judged by the equality and quality of life of the women in that society.

It is ironic that the break between Malcolm and Elijah was triggered due to Elijah's sexual exploitation of young black women when Malcolm was made aware that Elijah had fathered several children by different young women followers without assenting to legal paternity and financial responsibility. When Malcolm confronted Elijah about his breach of sexual ethics Elijah purportedly replied that a great man such as himself (Elijah) was not expected to conform to conventional sexual ethics. He instructed Malcolm about the great men of the Bible who also had participated in sexual activity that was outside of traditional sexual boundaries. These statements were reminiscent of the biblical defenses used by some of the Christaun ministers I had encountered.

However, Malcolm was unconvinced by his spiritual leader, and this breach of sexual ethics helped Malcolm to loosen the ties that bound him to Elijah Muhammad's philosophy and group. It was quite a shock to Malcolm to discover that his teacher and savior was guilty of the same breaches of sexual ethics for which he had publicly condemned hypocritical Christian preachers. Malcolm had lived a life of sexual purity as a Muslim minister and husband only to find that his leader had little regard for the sexual ethics he had taught his followers.

It was the issue of sexual ethics that also served as the tie that bound Malcolm to Elijah in the first place. During Malcolm's initial conversion to Islam while he was in prison his brother was censored by Elijah for sexual impropriety. Malcolm was sorely grieved for he had to choose between Elijah or his brother who had provided emotional support while he was in prison. His brother had also helped him gain membership into the Nation of Islam. In his autobiography Malcolm reports seeing an epiphany of the founder of the Nation; W. D. Fard, as he pondered which road he should take. It was this vision that was stimulated by his emotional crisis occasioned by his brother's suspension from the Nation of Islam that convinced Malcolm of his duty to Elijah Muhammad. That is why it is the greatest of ironies that Malcolm would later make a break with Elijah over the same issue that had occasioned his full allegiance to Elijah and the Nation of Islam.

Like Martin Luther King, Jr., we once again have the specter of a African American charismatic religious figure, in this case Elijah Muhammad, whose sexual ethics did not conform to his teaching. Unlike King, Elijah did produce a theological and ethical justification for his actions, although it apparently held no intellectual or moral currency with the extremely devout Malcolm X. This situation once again draws attention to the development and practice of a sexual ethic that is a reflection of a rapetalistic social situation that exploits black women and girls. Certainly Elijah's failure to take care of the children that his sexual unions created cannot be defended. Malcolm met with several of his sexual partners in attempts to help them gain paternity rights against Elijah and thereby further cemented his alienation from Elijah. In my nomenclature we are still struggling with an ethics that has been constructed between The Spirituals and The Blues.

Interracial Relationships

The subject of sexual ethics in the African American community cannot be complete without some consideration of the efficacy of interracial relationships. Here once again the ideas and practices of Malcolm and Martin serve as important starting points for this discussion. It can be said unequivocally that the end of their lives and ministry that both Malcolm and Martin believed that interracial liaisons were a private matter of the heart. Both men struggled with this issue and came to the same conclusions by different roads. Although they believed that these were private matters they were tolerant of interracial relationships for others even as they affirmed their need and desire for marriage to African American women. An examination of their lives in this context is an illustration of the irrationality and power of racism in America. Ironically if not for racism they both may have married white women since some of their deepest adult attachments were to white females.

Martin met and dated a white woman while he was in Seminary at Crozer, now Colgate Rochester Divinity School. In fact, Martin "stole" his girlfriend from one of his white instructors and closest friends on the campus. Although he was deeply in love with this woman he was warned against marriage because it would mean the end of his acceptance in the African American church community. Despite a very universal position in most social areas he black church has taken a much more narrow view regarding African American male-white female relationships. Martin understood that if he was to return to the South and minister to his people then marriage to a white woman would seriously curtail the possibilities of his employment by African American churches in the South, not to mention the attitudes and laws against miscegenation in the Jim Crow South.

Much of the white separatist propaganda of that time was directed toward the fear of African American males who were thought to desire white women as the ultimate goal of integration. King would have been a target of segregationists as well as African American church persons. Segregationists would have criticized him as a sex crazed African American male who used his affluence and power to gain sexual access to white women. In many states it was also unlawful for African Americans to marry white women and it would definitely have been a constant danger for a African American man and white women to be seen in each other's company

The African American community also expects its clergy to be role models for the community. Therefore a African American male who marries outside of the race is seen as not having the proper respect for African American women. I have often heard African American women say that if a African American man wants a white woman there are plenty of light skinned African American women for him to choose from. King understood that his liaison would have to come to an end if he was to be an effective minister in the African American community. After much thought and personal anguish he broke off the relationship for the sake of his higher calling. It is supremely ironic that King's fight for integration was made possible because he denied himself the same choices that he fought to uphold for others. This is one reason why it is difficult to make hard and fast universal rules regarding sexual ethics in the African American community. Universal rules of behavior are difficult to maintain when viewed in the context of the struggle for human freedom and equality. King's call to lead his people took precedence over his belief in the rights of persons to become sexually involved and marry without regard to race.

Malcolm, as was mentioned previously, was also sexually involved with white women. He admits in his autobiography how he was part of a African American male culture that sought white women as a prize; as forbidden fruit that was denied by whites to African American males. His actions and those of his friends were an act of defiance as much as they were an act of love as African American males sought out white women for sexual experiences. It is difficult however to remain at the purely physical sexual level in any relationship and it is obvious that Malcolm grew fond of his white paramour. He seems to have genuine sympathy for his white friend and doesn't blame her for his imprisonment but rightly sees it as a vindictive act by a white male patriarchal system which sentenced him for his sexual contact with white females.

After his conversion to the Nation of Islam Malcolm was able to honestly face the self-hatred that turned many African American males to seek after sexual companionship with white women. His new found pride in African beauty allowed him to rise above his previous behavior and help other African American men to face the demonic side of the sexual attraction they had for white women. However, it was only after his trip to Mecca and final conversion to orthodox Islam that Malcolm could state that who one chose to marry was a private affair. He had moved from his African American separatist position in which intermarriage with whites was forbidden to a universalistic position.

Unfortunately, we don't know as much about the nature of King's sexual attraction to white women so once again we can only speculate. We know that he was sexually active with both African American and white women although he seemed to be especially attracted to fine African American women who were given the title of "Doctors" by King and his cronies. The taboo against interracial dating and marriage between African American men and white women has gathered strength in the African American community as fewer African American males are available for marriage due to a lack of employment, incarceration and interracial dating. The African American church still expects its male clergy to marry within the race and I know of no prominent African American male preachers who are not married to African American women.

This is not true however of other African American male professionals who seem to choose nonwhite women almost as a matter of course. As long as white males continue to exercise the strongest taboo of all, i.e., white male marriages to African American women, there will continue to be severe shortages of eligible males to marry African American women. Thid taboo also exists for black female intermarriage to males of other ethnic groups in the United States.

Is the African American church correct in its stance regarding interracial marriage and represents a lingering commitmnt to black pride and black male-female solidarity? How do we develop a sexual ethic that is grounded in theological principles of freedom and equality but reserve the right to limit the marital choices of African American males? The situation that Martin Luther King found himself in is similar to the situation that many African American males now face. The African American community is so desperate for positive African American male role models that the argument favoring the need for African American males to marry within the race still carries a great deal of force.

From this perspective African American males should be counseled to think long and hard before deciding to marry outside of the race. However, if that is their choice the African American community should seek to incorporate them and their families into the black community. This would seem to be in keeping with the personal philosophies of both Malcolm and Martin. It may be that many African American males marry white women out of a racialized ideology of white supremacy that privileges the choice of white females as more suitable marriage partners. Instead of personal preference and attraction this would be a continuation of a rapetalistic society in which white supremacy, economic and class advantage promotes an ideology of black self hatred.

Regardless, the African American community cannot afford to cut off some of its most talented members because they are involved in relationships that involve non Black women.

In some cases it may be the easy way out for African American males to marry African American women because it protects them from undue criticism from their community. Paradoxically they may feel that marriage to a non-African American woman may be their way of seeking out of a perceived responsibility to the African American community. It may be a way of seeking to deny their African American-ness or declare a more universal perspective on life. In King's case it would be interesting to explore Coretta Scott King's attitude toward Martin's previous love for a white female. Did she consider herself to be a second choice for Martin's affections. Did this in any way fuel Martin's inability to remain faithful to her? I doubt that a black woman would feel loved knowing that her partner views her as a consolation prize for the woman he really wanted to marry.

Finally, love may be inexplicable and like the Spirit it blows where it wills. Except for those of us who chose to answer a higher calling, a calling that may no longer be necessary if racism can be obliterated, the best course it to encourage love and respect for all women. However, since the reality of media and popular culture devalues African American women it is also imperative that young African American males be taught that their African American sisters are just as special and desirous as any women that the rapetalistic American society raises as its standard of ultimate beauty and favor. If African American men marry white women because they have developed an idea that African American women are less than white, Hispanic or Asian women, then racism wins again and we all lose.

The final chapter will propose a set of ethical guidelines that can elicit thought and dialogue concerning human sexuality and sexual ethics in the black community. It is meant as a beginning point for further discussion and illumination regarding sexual ethics in the black community.

Chapter Four

Eight Rules to Live By: Love Does No Harm

A new command I give you: Love one another.
As I have loved you, so you must love one
another. St. John 13:34 NIV

All things are lawful, but not all things are profitable.
All things are lawful, but not all things
edify. 1 Corinthians 10:23NASB

The challenge that the African American churches, mosques, temples and synagogues face is how to develop a sexual ethic that is true to its most cherished beliefs, attitudes and practices. But even more important is the development of a sexual ethic that is consistent with the meaning of love as it appears in the highest aspirations in the numerous black religious traditions. It is too easy to lay down a restrictive morality that one assumes will allow for the expression of sexuality in a safe and responsible manner. The problem is that this kind of ethic often rebounds against itself because few persons can keep the rules that have been developed for another place and another time. Often the rules are used to make others fell guilty and, in the words of Jesus, create loads that people cannot bear.

The Apostle Paul, who in 1 Cor. 6 warns against sexual immorality, was convinced that celibacy was the truest form of sexual practice. His overly restrictive views were influenced by a social world in which women were the objects of sexual exploitation and denigration that in turn was linked to the worship of the gods of the socially powerful. His vociferous condemnation of the Corinthians ould easily br read as a condemnation of bodily hedonism and an unfettered egoism that could only be expressed in the Greco-Roman cultural worship of other gods. Gods who were only served by a selfish attitude of sexual consumption by the rich and powerful. Pau's condemnation of the unequal distribution of the agape meal in his letter to the Corinthians is another indication of his attempt to create a community based on equal regard and a care for the poor.

Anyone who states that today's Christians must refrain from sexual immorality solely based on the writings of the New Testament must also abide with the teachings of Jesus that states that divorce is only permitted on the basis of infidelity, a position which Jesus probably held in order to protect women from the whims of males who could divorce their spouses without due cause. The important thing to remember is that under grace we are to base our ethical decisions on the principle of love for God, self and the neighbor. This means that any rules, including the ones that follow, are always subject to revision based on the necessities created by love.

The Rules:

One
Know thyself.

The ideal of knowing oneself was the primary commandment of the ancient world. It preceded the commandment to love and is inextricably linked to love as the Egyptian Imhotep and the Greek Socrates admonished their followers to gain knowledge of self. Who are you? How do you feel about yourself? What we call self-identity and self-esteem issues must be considered in the development of the person who wished to connect in the most intimate of ways with other persons.

When the Bible uses the metaphor of knowing to stand for the act of sexual activity it is referring this ancient rule; for it is in our sexual relationships that we have the greatest possibility of knowing and being known by others. Sexuality is a part of the fabric of human identity and self-esteem. We are created by the process of sexual knowing be it in love, knowledge, hatred or indifference. We are affected by this process whether we know it or not. The best sex occurs when persons feel as though they are being truly known and held in high regard by their sexual partner.

One must know who they are in order to be in a relationship successfully with someone else. One must understand the makeup of their sexual person. Are they straight or gay? Are they masculine or feminine? How sexual are they? These matters and others involving our identity will influence the quality of the sexual relationship. We should know who we are and what we like when it comes to issues of sexuality and sexual functioning. The ability to communicate that to your partner is an essential part of the relationship.

No person is absolutely masculine or feminine, straight or gay, erotic or unmoved by sexual passion. Our sexuality changes over time as well. As we grow older we may either see the wisdom of being less sexual or grow to be more comfortable with our sexuality. As men grow older they appreciate the more feminine aspects of their personality just as females are more willing to express their more masculine tendencies. The most important thing is to be in constant contact of who we have been, who we are and where we are evolving in our sexual being.

Two
Thou shall love one another as you love yourself.

Agape or Christian love must be the foundation of a fulfilling sexual relationship. Christian love is the kind of love that is willing to serve others. As we know who we are we become able to better fill the needs of those around us. Since we can know and ask for what we need sexually we can return the favor to our loved ones.

The key word is respect. This means regard for the lover and a willingness to put their needs before one's own when it is called for. We are able to honor and serve our partners knowing that we reap what we sow. If we want love then we must give love without conditions or reservations. Giving your mate sexual pleasure is a special part of the relationship. Communicate about what is pleasant and exciting. The use of sex manuals, movies, etc. are important tools to accomplish this goal. Touching lovingly and tenderly is the foundation of knowing your partner.

If we feel taken advantage of in our loving of another person then it is important to know this and to communicate this to your partner. As the apostle wrote; all things are possible but not all things build up and edify the spirit. It is important to feel that you receive as well as give in a relationship that is mutually loving.

When there are differences in attitudes about what feels comfortable, appropriate and loving it is important to discuss the situation and to explore options. No two people are likely to agree on everything but there needs to be a space created where honesty can prevail. At first I was surprised how many couples had hidden their true feelings about their partner's lovemaking in fear that egos would be bruised. Sexual relationships should be looked at as an educational experience for both parties as they travel in their journey together. It is important to at least be open to new horizons and to not be afraid of being criticized in a healthy manner. We can only learn how to please one another by stating the pros and cons of various sexual experiences.

Three
Thou shall love thy body as a gift from God.

It is important not to fall into the historical trap of being overly spiritual or overly bluesy. The traditional sexual ethics of Africans was regulated by a sense of responsibility both economically and socially.

The primary function of sexuality was to increase the human population and to give pleasure. The sexual act has the power to increase the emotional bonds between partners. The pleasure of sexuality can serve to strengthen and reinforce the sense of closeness in the family.

In most cultures sexuality was permitted between persons who were economically stable and emotionally suited for each other. Those two factors of money and emotional compatibility are often overlooked in today's rush for instant gratification so that we often choose one over the other instead of looking for both. The ancient wisdom of having families arrange marriages was a way of ensuring that both needs were met.

It is also important-to shed notions that the body is nasty and sinful. Masturbation; touching oneself in a sexual manner through stroking and rubbing oneself and others; is an important tool for understanding the body and its sexually exciting places. In order to know oneself one must know and love one's body. Masturbation can be an expression of self-knowledge and love.

I have found a disturbing ignorance among African American men and women regarding the psychological, anatomical and physiological conditions of sexual pleasure. In some cases I have been told by young women that if they were to demonstrate a higher level of sexual knowledge than their male partner they would be looked upon as being sexually loose. They therefore did not engage in sexual educational activities in order to allow their eventual mates to teach them about sexual behavior.

Hopefully, this tendency to stay ignorant of sexual knowledge will decrease as well as the previously documented hesitance that African American men and women have regarding sexual experimentation. This returns us to knowing one's sexual needs and being willing to tell them to one's partner. Several women and women have told me that they did not know what their partner wanted from them sexually until it was too late to repair their relationship as their partners sought sexual fulfillment with persons outside of their relationship who were willing to engage in sexual experimentation.

Four
Thou Shall Maintain Professional Boundaries

African American clergy and other helping professionals must be careful to maintain appropriate physical and emotional boundaries with those with who they have developed a close relationship with during times of personal and social crisis. One of my close friends and counselors taught me about the difficulty she observed with African American male counselors in keeping appropriate boundaries with their clients.

I have seen African American therapists; male and female, develop inappropriate relationships with their clients as they have become more concerned with being their friends instead of their counselors. This often resulted in a lack of objectivity as the healing relationship was substituted to satisfy the needs for friendship of the client or counselor.

It is important that the clergy or helping professional get their personal and sexual needs met by others so that this does not become an issue for the pastor, the helping professional, or the parishioner/client.

Five
African American men shall love African American women first and foremost.

It is an unfortunate social fact that the social oppression experienced by African American males has depleted the number of marriageable African American males so that the odds of African American women finding suitable partners continues to diminish. This would not be a problem if a sizeable number of non-African American males were open to dating and marrying African American females, but this is not the case. Non white males are not encouraged to be open to relationships with African American females. This attitude persists even though some small changes have occurred.

I was teaching on one liberal campus where students challenged each other to engage in interracial dating. Students were upbraided if they only dated persons of their own race or ethnic group. This meant that African American males were encouraged to date nonAfrican American women which resulted in most of the African American women not dating for their four years on the campus. The students, in their liberal zeal, had forgotten that African American females were already facing limited opportunities for intimate relationships due to the dearth of African American men on campus and that the White, Asian and Hispanic males were not open to dating African American women. These males dated non-African American females and still met the expectations of their liberal/progressive classmates.

It is true that you can't help who you fall in love with but African American men should remember African American women have sustained us through slavery and discrimination and loved us when no one else would. Now that African American men are an endangered species African American men should give priority to loving and marrying African American women. This love cannot be commanded but should be freely given, not as obligation but as a celebration.

Six
Thou shall practice safe sex and only bring children into the world that you can love and take care of emotionally and financially.

Responsible means of birth control will be practiced to prevent the arrival of unwanted children. Unwanted or unwise pregnancies are the biggest stumbling block to the future of our community. Sexually transmitted diseases, including AIDS are destroying the lives and reproductive abilities of many African Americans. Condoms should be worn at all times especially if the couple has not been tested for sexually transmitted diseases and there is the possibility of multiple partners. Lovers should learn how to please each other without sexual penetration as the only option or goal of love making. There are a myriad of ways that lovers can experience sexual pleasure without the need for sexual penetration.

Seven
Thou shall love thy gay, lesbian, bisexual, transgendered neighbor like thyself.

The African American community must no longer fall prey to the false standards of patriarchal bias and heterosexist discrimination that comes from a threatened Patriarchal masculinity. It must educate itself to the biblical interpretations regarding human sexuality that have not been affected by a patriarchal ideology that has distorted the meaning of sexuality and Christian love. We must develop more faithful interpretations regarding sexuality and be critical of outdated judgments and biases that are no longer applicable to our day and time. We will recognize that the first Non Jewish Christian in the Bible was the Ethiopian Eunuch: a man of African descent and of a different sexual orientation. He was also the servant of one of the African American queens of Ethiopia. We were brought into the Kingdom of God as full members who represent the diversity and equality of all God's creation regardless of race, color or sexual orientation.

The down low phenomenon in the African American community has harmed African American men, women and families. Because African American men don't want to limit their chances of having a family and risk the social stigmatization of being seen as homosexual they have developed a practice of lying to potential mates and spouses. This has led to increasing levels of HIV-AIDS infections among African American women who have had and are having sex with their partners without realizing that they may be having sex with men who are not protecting themselves from HIV infection. This situation is extremely destructive to the physical and spiritual security of African American women and families. Gay males must take responsibility for their sexual attitudes and behaviors so that at the very least they will not engage in high risk sexual behaviors with other males and do everything possible to protect their spouses from infection.

In the meantime the African American community must come to terms with the meaning of homosexual sexuality and begin to develop a non-punitive and appreciative stance toward those persons whom God has created gay. It is tragic that a community that has experienced so much oppression due to its biological differences in terms of skin color would penalize others who are "naturally" different as well.

Eight
No Abuse-Love Does No Harm

Any relationship that is based on hurting someone else is wrong and should be avoided, terminated and reported if it continues. There can be no room in a Christian Ethic of Love for relationships in which persons are being physically, psychologically or emotionally abused. The human spirit was meant to soar, not demeaned and limited by persons who would use others solely for their own needs.

The abuser often tries to silence the victim or even to convince them that they are responsible for the abusive relationship. The abuser may threaten or try and convince them that without this relationship the person would have no relationship at all. It is in the abuser's self-interest to convince the victim that they are not worthy of love.

However, love does no harm. A relationship that is based on humiliation, degradation and exploitation is not love but represents a deep sickness of the human soul. My wish for the reader is that they will find a relationship that is worthy of their status as the children of God.

Epilogue

This book has been a first attempt a addressing the issue of sexual abuse in the Black Churches. Because the churches are also an important institution it also has implications for questions regarding sexual ethics in the larger Black community. My hope is that this is just the beginning salvo in ending an abusive process that has robbed so many African Americans of their personal spiritual and psychological safety. When religious leaders fail to exercise appropriate restraint and adopt abusive practices within their church and community the harm that exists can have long lasting effects from generation to generation. I hope that one of the major factors as to why this problem is so pervasive was made clear by my historical, analysis of the ethical positions within the Black Church and community. Along with the anti-psychological bias in the black community, the black church has developed a discourse which promotes and hides the awful facts of sexual abuse. It is time to develop an ethical discourse that identifies and prevents this sexual misconduct. This will take a reevaluation of the traditional values in which patriarchal power and inequality have led to this culture of violence and abuse.

Appendix

African/African American Ethics

African Response To Tragedy *Before American Captivity-Pre-1619*	African American Response To Tragedy *From 1640'S To 1885*	African American Response To Tragedy *Post Reconstruction-1885-Present*
led to:	led to:	led to:
The Traditional Ethic: Providence And Fate *Appollo-Dionysian Ethics*	**The Spiritual Ethic: Transforming Tragedy** *Appollonian Ethics*	**The Blues Ethic: Accepting Tragedy** *Dionysian Ethics*
Desire to maintain cultural patterns	Desire for order and protection from sexual exploitation. Slaveholders-illegal polygamy of sexual hedonism for procreation and profit.	Desire for individual freedom in the face of hopelessness. Forced sex thru violence and coercion. Lynching, torture

The Traditional: Sexual Ethic Of Embodied Spirituality	**The Spiritual: Sexual Ethic Of Family Regard**	**The Blues: Sexual Ethic Of Erotic Joy**
Cultural Harmony and Balance between order and sensuality.	Ethic of Discretion and Sexual Restraint	Ethic of Pleasure and Sensuality

The Traditional: Sexual Ethic Of Embodied Spirituality	The Spiritual: Sexual Ethic Of Family Regard	The Blues: Sexual Ethic Of Erotic Joy
Sexual Practices-Legal polygamy	Blacks-Resistance to sexual exploitation thru ritual practices (jumping the broom) and legal monogamy.	Blacks-Exploitation of Sexuality based on bodily hedonism and psychological egoism
Male and Female Religious leaders	Male suppression	Black Romanticism
Ascending Patriarchy-Fuedalism; Islamic and Christian	Female leadership resisted and affirmed-Black Matriarchy as social necessity.	Re-Emerging female empowerment. Black Womanist

Acknowledgments

**To All Those Who Were Brave Enough To Tell Their Story
May The Ancestors
Be Honored By This Work**

I have appreciated the support of many persons over the more than fifteen years I have taught, thought and written about these matters. The African American Graduate Forum at the University of Chicago served as the genesis for many of the ideas expressed in the book, especially the concept of Rapetalistic (racial, sexual and economic) oppression. Brothers and sisters like Stephen Casmier, Matthew Johnson, Ted Manley, Lee Cornelius, Antonio "Tkufu" McDaniel, Annette Collins, Michelle Briggs, and Angela Harris strongly influenced many of these ideas as we "kicked it" at the C' Shop.

The first class that I taught on Human Sexuality and the African American Community was at Chicago Theological Seminary seventeen years ago where students like Rev. Diana Brady Timberlake, Rev. Booker Vance, Rev. Dr. Marcellous Mack, Rev. Zenobia Brooks, Rev. Dr. Sharon Ellis and many others played important roles in shaping my ideas about sexualized stigma in the African American churches.

I also found support within the official walls of academia from Archie Smith Jr., James Gustafson, John Comaroff, Jean Comaroff, David Tracy and Lauren Berlant who became more than academic advisors as they allowed and encouraged me to speak the truth to power in the academic setting.

I owe a debt of gratitude to the Religion Departments of Central Michigan and Temple Universities and colleagues like Roger Hatch, Merlyn Mowery and John Raines who gave me the space to speak the unspeakable in presentations and papers. This work could not have continued without the early support of African American womanists, theologians, social scientists and ethicists like Cheryl Townsend Gilkes, Sheila Briggs and Joan Martin. They gave me the initial encouragement to consider their various perspectives on gender and race.

My colleagues at Colgate Rochester Divinity School and the Chicago Consortium including James Poling, Evelyn Kirkley, Lois Livezy, Walter Fluker and Susan Thistlethwaite allowed me to explore these topics in various classes and lectures at Colgate Rochester Divinity School and Chicago Theological Seminary. Versions of this work were presented at sessions sponsored by the Afro-American, Women and Religion, Narrative Theology and Ethics Sections of the Annual Meeting of the American Academy of Religion. Professors William Placher and Naomi Goldenberg are to be thanked for their early recognition of my work.

My ministerial colleagues; Rev. Dr. Donald F. Guest, Rev. William Vance, and Sister Esther Belle Henderson, guided me through my formative years and were profound spiritual influences on my life and work. Dr. Guest was the first to hip me to the latent hypocrisy of African American church sexual ethics. Other academic colleagues; Thabiti Lewis, Josef Sorett, Linda Perkins, Adam Clark, Elonda Clay, Paula McGee, Merlyn Mowery, Joyce Baugh, Linda Thomas and Joyce Williams asked hard questions that helped me to refine my thesis. I alone am responsible for the content and nature of this work.

This book was begun in 1993 while I was a postdoctoral fellow at the African and African American and Religious Studies Departments at Washington University in St. Louis. A special thanks goes to Gerald Early and Patout Burns who invited me to work and teach as the first Post-Doctoral Fellow in African and African American Studies at Wash U. Adele Tuechler and Raye Riggins helped provide a suitable environment and a helpful hand as I pondered the nature of this academic discourse.

A most special thanks goes to my sisters and students at Wash U., St. Louis University and the University of Missouri at Kansas City. Allison Francis, Rebecka Rutledge, Dessie Fisher, Deborah Foster, the late Pamela Shane Dillard, Tiffanie Foster, Ruby Watson, Toni Choate, Brenda Gardner, Jane Cannon and a host of African American women challenged me and helped me to keep it real from the perspective of African American lay women. A special thanks to my running buddies Deb and Thabiti for providing constant encouragement, both material and spiritual in support of this book.

The opportunity to teach classes on sexuality and the African American community at Chicago Theological Seminary, Colgate Rochester Divinity School, Washington University at St. Louis, St. Louis University, the University of California at Santa Cruz and the University of Missouri at Kansas City, where I directed the African American Studies Program, were invaluable in helping me to refine my ideas on sexuality and the African American community. Drs. Stewart Sigman, Stuart Lord and Carol Blackshire-Belay of Naropa University provided resources to complete the manuscript. Janine Ibbotson and Liz Acosta provided the grace and space.

I owe a major debt of gratitude to the women of my tribe: my mother Ada, sister; Carole, Nana Esther, "Aint" Amandy and the other deceased women like Sweet Mama Ada and her mother, Sarah, the first of our clan freed from American slavery. They influenced me from above the veil and were influential and abiding spiritual presences during the research and writing of this book.

My nieces and nephews: Tanya, Annie, Tracye, Gerald, Lisa, Eric, and Andrea taught me about the challenges that this generation still faces. My greatest thanks goes to my sister; Rev. Mary Thompson, who hosted and cared for me during the final revision of this manuscript. She along with my children; Jonathan, William, Joanna, Faith, Jon, son-in-law John Paun, Merlyn Mowery and Myklos Ferber, Aunt Johnetta, Uncle Martin, Ruby Russell of St. Marks Church, Kansas City, MO, Rev. Dr. Emmanuel Akognon and members of Village Baptist Church, Marin City CA, my brother Dr. Alvin Matthews and Joanna Farmer provided the sustenance and inspiration with space, food, fellowship and concern during my time of personal struggles and peril.

Finally, I hope that my grandchildren; Janessa, Juliana, Jasmine, plus one more J on the way, will benefit from these words. For I hope they will give impetus for the creation of a more ethical world in which they might live and prosper.

Donald Henry Matthews, PhD.
Boulder, CO 2012

CPSIA information can be obtained
at www.ICGtesting.com
Printed in the USA
BVHW070828290821
615482BV00001B/59